WAYNE GISSLEN

STUDY GUIDE
TO ACCOMPANY
PROFESSIONAL
COOKING

SEVENTH EDITION

WILEY

JOHN WILEY & SONS, INC.

Published by John Wiley & Sons, Inc., Hoboken, New Jersey
Published simultaneously in Canada.

Library of Congress Cataloging-in-Publication Data:

ISBN: 978-0-470-19751-6

Printed in the United States of America

10 9 8 7 6 5 4 3 2 1

To the Student

This *Study Guide* is a companion to *Professional Cooking,* seventh edition. Its purpose is to help you study and review the material in the text.

Learning to cook is primarily a practical, hands-on endeavor. It is, for the most part, a matter of learning manual skills by practicing them under the guidance of an instructor or supervisor, and then improving those skills by repeated practice.

These practical skills, however, depend on a large body of knowledge and understanding. You need to know about cooking theory, basic procedures, general guidelines, and ingredient information. Using this manual will help you to study and to master this material.

This *Study Guide* is arranged by chapter, corresponding to the 35 chapters in *Professional Cooking*. Each chapter contains several exercises that you can use to test your own knowledge. Then you can see what you have learned and what you need to review. The following are guidelines for using the different kinds of exercises.

Chapter Goals

These are the same goals that appear at the beginning of each text chapter. They are not exercises, but they are included here as a reminder of the specific skills you should be learning in each chapter.

Terms

The first exercise in each chapter is a list of definitions or descriptions of terms used in the kitchen. In each of the blanks provided, write the term that is defined or described. (In Chapter 3, some of the questions in the terms section ask you to identify a picture; give the name of the item in the illustration. You will find more questions asking you to identify pictures in some other chapters.)

This is the only kind of exercise you will find in every chapter. Why is there so much emphasis on terms? It is important not only that you learn how to cook but that you can communicate with other cooks. A food service career involves teamwork and sharing of information. To communicate, you must know the language of the kitchen.

True/False Questions

For each question, draw a circle around the T if the statement is completely true. Draw a circle around the F if the statement is only partly true or is completely false.

Completion, Short-Answer Questions, and Other Written Exercises

Many exercises ask you to fill in blanks with words or phrases or to write out various kinds of answers.

If the problem is a straight question, a space is provided for you to write out the answer.

If the problem is a statement that contains one or more blanks, fill in the blanks so that the statement is true and makes a complete sentence.

If the problem asks you to write a procedure or to explain how to do a task, write out the procedure using numbered steps. You do not need to *explain* each step, the way the text sometimes does, but be sure that your procedure is complete. Don't leave out any steps.

Math Exercises

Math is very important in the professional kitchen. Throughout your career you will have to make many kinds of mathematical calculations. Some of the most basic of these are explained in *Professional Cooking*.

In Chapter 5, you learn how to do the following kinds of math:

Handling units of measure
Working with food cost percentages
Performing yield tests
AP/EP yields
Converting recipe yields
Calculating portion costs

The last two of these are so important that you will find exercises throughout this manual to give you practice.

Other kinds of math problems are explained in Chapter 29. Whenever you have difficulty with any of the math problems, turn to the explanation in the text and review it.

Note that math exercises using units of measure appear twice, once with U.S. units and once with metric units. Complete whichever exercises your instructor asks you to do.

These are the kinds of exercises you will find most often in this manual. There are also other kinds of problems and questions that are especially included to help you review the material in a particular chapter. The instructions at the beginning of each of these sections explain how to do the problems.

Contents

STUDY GUIDE
TO ACCOMPANY
PROFESSIONAL
COOKING

Chapter 1

The Food-Service Industry

This chapter gives you a general picture of modern food service and a look at the history of the profession. There is not much technical information that you have to memorize, but there are some important concepts that you should be familiar with. These questions will help you review.

After studying Chapter 1, you should be able to:

1. Name and describe four major developments that have significantly changed the food-service industry in the twentieth century.

2. Identify seven major stations in a classical kitchen.

3. Explain how the size and type of an operation influence the organization of the modern kitchen.

4. Identify and describe three skill levels of food production personnel.

5. Identify eight behavioral characteristics that food service workers should develop and maintain to achieve the highest standards of professionalism.

A. Terms

Fill in each blank with the term that is defined or described.

head chef/executive   **1.** The person in charge of the kitchen.

Garde Manager   **2.** The person responsible for preparing cold foods, such as salads, salad dressings, and cold hors d'oeuvres.

_____ **3.** French term for a new style of cooking, developed mainly in the 1970s, especially popular in France.

_____ **4.** The chef who is sometimes known as the father of twentieth-century cooking and considered the greatest chef of his age (he died in 1935).

_____ 5. The person responsible for preparing vegetables, starches, soups, and eggs.

_____ 6. The person responsible for preparing sauces, sautéed foods, and stews.

__Relief_____ 7. The person who replaces other station chefs when they are absent.

_____ 8. The French chef who is considered the greatest chef of the early nineteenth century; he refined and organized cooking, and he was also famous for creating elaborate display pieces.

_____ 9. The person responsible for preparing roasted and braised meats.

_____ 10. The person responsible for preparing desserts and pastries.

_____ 11. A varied set of scientific techniques used by avant-garde chefs, including the uses of nonstandard chemical and physical processes in cooking.

_____ 12. In a large establishment, the person who is responsible for all aspects of food production, including menu planning, purchasing, costing, and planning work schedules; in other words, the manager of a large kitchen.

_____ 13. The person who reports to the person described in number 12, and who directly manages the kitchen production staff.

_____ 14. The person who is in charge of the kitchen and who also works at one or more of the production stations, usually in smaller establishments.

_____ 15. A set of techniques for cooking vacuum-packed foods at precise temperatures.

_____ 16. A person who is in charge of one particular area of production in a kitchen.

_____ 17. A set of attitudes and code of behavior followed by successful food-service workers.

B. Matching

Column 1 below lists some of the items prepared by the kitchen of a certain hotel. Column 2 lists the titles of the station cooks. In the blanks provided before each food item, write the letter from column 2 which corresponds to the title of the cook who prepares it.

_____	1. Roast beef top round	a. Saucier
_____	2. White wine sauce	b. Entremetier
_____	3. Chocolate cream pie	c. Rotisseur
_____	4. Trout amandine	d. Garde Manger
_____	5. Broiled veal chops	e. Grillardin
_____	6. Waldorf salad	f. Poissonier
_____	7. Braised veal shoulder	g. Patissier
_____	8. Lamb stew	h. Aboyeur

_____   **9.** Canapés

_____   **10.** Blue cheese dressing

_____   **11.** Boiled potatoes

_____   **12.** Roast chicken with gravy

_____   **13.** Split pea soup

_____   **14.** Fried breaded shrimp

_____   **15.** Beef stew

_____   **16.** Chicken liver pâté

_____   **17.** Baked apples

_____   **18.** Sautéed veal scaloppine

_____   **19.** Steamed broccoli

_____   **20.** Poached halibut steaks

C. True/False

T   F   **1.** The position of short-order cook is an entry-level job, because it requires no skills or experience.

T   F   **2.** Institutional kitchens like school cafeterias usually do more cooking to order than restaurants do.

T   F   **3.** Because modern technology uses so many new chemicals, food poisoning is more of a danger today than it was a hundred years ago.

T   F   **4.** The word *chef* is a French term meaning *cook*.

T   F   **5.** Because more and more people are beginning to appreciate fresh foods, convenience foods are becoming less important in food-service kitchens.

T   F   **6.** Teamwork is not important in a restaurant where most dishes are cooked to order, because each cook completes his or her own specific tasks.

T   F   **7.** Good restaurants have high menu prices, because high-quality food always costs more to prepare than poor or average food.

T   F   **8.** The *tournant* is the cook who is responsible for preparing foods on a rotisserie.

T   F   **9.** The organization of the kitchen staff depends in part on whether foods are mostly cooked to order or mostly prepared ahead in large quantities.

T   F   **10.** Because of the new styles of cooking developed in the past 25 years, the old techniques of the so-called "classical cooking" are no longer used.

T   F   **11.** The Berkeley, California restaurant Chez Panisse, which pioneered the use of seasonal, locally grown, organic foods, was started by Alice Waters.

T   F   **12.** The word *restaurant* is derived from a French word meaning *fortifying* or *restorative*.

T   F   **13.** Modern restaurants are generally considered to have begun when a Parisian named Boulanger began selling soup.

T   F   **14.** The main difference between professional cooking and home cooking is that professional cooking relies on recipes for larger quantities.

T   F   **15.** The style of cooking called *sous vide* was developed largely by Spanish chef Ferran Adrià.

T   F   **16.** Training in culinary arts is good preparation for a great variety of jobs not only in food service but in other pursuits as well.

Chapter 2

Sanitation and Safety

Good sanitation and safety practices must underlie all your work as a food-service professional. The exercises in this chapter help to reinforce your understanding of sanitation and food-borne diseases, especially because sanitation is the subject of many laws and regulations governing this industry.

After studying Chapter 2, you should be able to:

1. Describe steps to prevent food poisoning and food-borne diseases in the following areas: personal hygiene, food handling and storage techniques, cleaning and sanitizing procedures, and pest control.

2. Identify safe workplace habits that prevent injuries from the following: cuts, burns, operation of machinery and equipment, and lifting.

3. Identify safe workplace habits that minimize the likelihood of fires and falls.

A. Terms

Fill in each blank with the term that is defined or described.

_____ 1. A food-borne disease caused by a parasite sometimes found in undercooked pork.

_____ 2. Any bacteria that can cause disease.

_____ 3. Any food-borne disease caused by toxins or poisons that are produced by bacteria while they are growing in food.

_____ 4. Any food-borne disease caused by organisms that get into the intestinal system and attack the body.

_____ 5. Any food-borne disease caused by organisms that get into the body and produce toxins as they grow in the body.

_____   **6.** A term that describes bacteria that grow when no air is present.

_____   **7.** A term that describes bacteria that can grow with or without the presence of air.

_____   **8.** The name for the temperature range in which disease-causing bacteria will grow easily.

_____   **9.** A term that describes bacteria that need air to grow.

_____   **10.** The period of time after bacteria come in contact with a food and before they start growing and multiplying.

_____   **11.** A substance that causes an allergic reaction in people.

_____   **12.** An organism that is larger than a bacteria and that can survive only by living on or inside another organism.

_____   **13.** A general term for diseases caused by such substances as lead, cyanide, and copper.

_____   **14.** Removing visible soil.

_____   **15.** Killing disease-causing bacteria.

_____   **16.** The transfer of disease-causing bacteria to food from another food or from equipment or work surfaces.

_____   **17.** The movement of food through a food-service operation.

_____   **18.** A food safety system usually known by the initials HACCP. (Write out the five-word name.)

_____

_____

_____

_____

_____   **19.** A risk that can lead to a dangerous condition in food; a term used in the system described in number 18.

_____   **20.** The last opportunity a worker has to control a particular hazard.

_____   **21.** Foods that provide a good environment for the growth of disease-causing microorganisms.

_____   **22.** Contamination of food with objects that may not be toxic but that may cause injury or discomfort.

_____   **23.** A substance that causes an allergic reaction.

B. Review of Food-Borne Diseases

Fill in the blanks as required.

1. *Botulism*

    a. Caused by what organism? _____

    b. What foods might carry it? _____

    _____

    c. How can it be prevented? _____

    _____

    _____

2. *Staph poisoning*

    a. Caused by what organism? _____

    b. What foods might carry it? _____

    _____

    _____

    c. How can it be prevented? _____

    _____

    _____

3. *Salmonella*

    a. Caused by what organism? _____

    b. What foods might carry it? _____

    _____

    _____

    c. How can it be prevented? _____

    _____

    _____

4. *Clostridium perfringens*

   a. Where do the disease-causing bacteria come from? _____

   _____

   b. What foods might carry the bacteria? _____

   _____

   _____

   c. How can the disease be prevented? _____

   _____

   _____

5. *Strep infection*

   a. Where do the disease-causing bacteria come from? _____

   _____

   b. What foods might carry the bacteria? _____

   _____

   _____

   c. How can the disease be prevented? _____

   _____

   _____

6. *Infectious hepatitis*

   a. Where do the disease-causing organisms come from? _____

   _____

   b. How can the disease be prevented? _____

   _____

7. *Trichinosis*

a. Where do the disease-causing organisms come from? _____

_____

b. How can the disease be prevented? _____

_____

8. *Escherichia coli*

a. Where do the disease-causing bacteria come from? _____

_____

b. What foods might carry the bacteria? _____

_____

_____

c. How can the disease be prevented? _____

_____

_____

C. Short-Answer Questions

1. What are the three basic ways to control bacteria that cause food-borne disease? _____

_____

_____

2. How are most food-borne disease bacteria spread? _____

_____

3. What are the two purposes of safe food storage? _____

_____

_____

4. Give three examples of times when food workers must wash their hands _____

_____

_____ .

5. Perishable foods must be held or stored at a temperature lower than _____ or higher than

_____ .

6. What is the recommended temperature for freezer storage? _____ .

7. List the four kinds of organisms that can contaminate food and cause illness.

_____

_____

_____

_____

8. What are the four basic methods of controlling insect and rodent infestations? _____

_____

_____

_____

9. What type of fire extinguisher do you need to put out a grease fire? _____

10. Discuss how the flow of food is considered when setting up a system for food safety. _____

_____

_____

_____

_____

11. As food flows from receiving to serving, what three categories of hazards can result in the food becoming

dangerous to eat? _____

_____

_____

12. What are the six categories of potentially hazardous foods (TCS Foods)? _____

_____

_____

_____

13. List the seven steps of the HACCP system.

_____

_____

_____

_____

_____

_____

_____

14. State the ideal storage temperatures for the following foods: Eggs _____ Raw celery _____

Whole milk _____ Whole raw fish _____ Raw chicken _____

15. Give two examples of plant toxins.

_____

_____

16. State the four-hour rule. _____

_____

_____

17. Give the minimum internal cooking temperatures and times for cooking the following foods:

Seafood: _____ for _____ seconds.

Ground beef: _____ for _____ seconds.

Roast chicken: _____ for _____ seconds.

Ham steaks: _____ for _____ seconds.

Venison chop: _____ for _____ seconds.

Beef roast: _____ for 4 minutes.

Beef roast: _____ for 12 minutes.

18. The four-hour rule means that _____

_____

_____

19. In the one-stage cooling method, you must cool a food to below 41°F (5°C) in no more than _____ hours.

20. The correct way to dry dishes after washing them is _____

_____

_____

Chapter 3

Tools and Equipment

Y ou might think of this chapter as a guide to the professional kitchen or as a catalog of basic equipment. The following exercises help you review your understanding of the tools you will be working with.

After studying Chapter 3, you should be able to:

Identify the do's and don'ts associated with the safe and efficient use of standard kitchen equipment; processing equipment; holding and storage equipment; measuring devices; and knives, hand tools, and small equipment.

A. Terms

For each of the first 10 questions, fill in the blank with the term that is described or defined. For questions 11 through 31, write the name of the items pictured and their most important uses in the blanks provided.

wood burning **1.** A type of oven that uses burning wood to provide smoke or heat or both.

bain-marie **2.** Another name for a hot-water bath.

Aluminum **3.** The most widely used metal for pots and pans used in restaurants.

dicer **4.** An attachment for mixers and food choppers, used to cut foods into cube shapes.

trunnion kettle **5.** A steam-jacketed kettle that can be tilted for emptying.

dough hook **6.** A mixer attachment used to mix and develop yeast doughs.

griddle **7.** A flat, smooth, metal surface on which food is cooked directly, such as pancakes, eggs, and hamburgers.

tang **8.** The portion of the metal knife blade that is inside the handle.

steel **9.** A sword-shaped tool used to true the edges of knives.

Rotisserie **10.** An item that cooks foods by turning them on spits in front of heating elements.

11.

Name of item: Stockpot w/ spigot

Major use: Allow liquid to drain w/out disturbing solid

12.

Name of item: Brazier (rondeau)

Major use: braising, braising, + stewing meats

13.

Name of item: Sauce pot/pan

Major use: Sauces

14.

Name of item: (Sateuse) Sautée pan (slop-sided)

Major use: Fry + sautée, easy flip

15.

Name of item: Sheet pan

Major use: baking & broiling meats

16.

Name of item: Roasting Pan

Major use: roasting meats & poultry

17.

Name of item: hotel pan, counter pan, steamtable pan, service pan

Major use: baking, steaming, & serving

18.

Name of item: liquid volume measure

Major use: pints, quarts, 1/2 gallons gallons liquid measure

19.

Name of item: Scoop

Major use: portioning solid foods

20.

Name of item: French/Chef's Knife

Major use: Chopping, slicing dicing etc.

21.

Name of item: boning knife

Major use: boning raw meats + poultry

22.

Name of item: Slicer

Major use: Carving + slicing meats

23.

Name of item: oyster knife

Major use: open oysters

24.

Name of item: Straight Spatula

Major use: Spread icing, mixing & bowl scraping

25.

Name of item: offset Spatula

Major use: lift eggs, meats, + pancakes off of grills, griddles, sheet pans etc.

26.

Name of item: Skimmer

Major use: Skim froth from liquids + renae solid pieces from soups stocks, etc

27.

Name of item: Wire whip/wisk

Major use: heavy for thick liquids - balloon for eggs cream hollandaise, + thinner liquids

28.

Name of item: _China cap_

Major use: _Used when great clarity or smoothness is needed in a liquid_

29.

Name of item: _Colander_

Major use: _drain washed or cooked veggies, salad greens, pasta, etc._

30.

Name of item: _Food mill_

Major use: _puréeing foods_

31.

Name of item: _Mandoline_

Major use: _cut/slice julienne or bâtonnet_

B. Knife Parts

In the illustration below, insert the name of each knife part in the blanks provided.

tang

spine

handle

tip

bolster

rivets

cutting edge

heel

C. True/False

T F   1. If an open gas burner doesn't light on first try, it's best to wait a minute before checking the pilot light and trying again.

T F   2. When filling a fry kettle with fresh solid shortening, it is best to set the thermostat to high (375°F or 190°C) until the fat is melted.

T **F**   3. Because of the air circulation in a convection oven, you need to set the temperature higher than for a regular oven.

T F   4. Pressure steamers must not be opened while the equipment is in operation.

T **F**   5. Paddle attachments for mixers are interchangeable and can be used with any size bowl.

T **F**   6. Stainless steel is an ideal material for cooking pots because it conducts heat well.

T F   7. Copper is a good material for pots and pans because it is a good heat conductor, but its disadvantages are that it is heavy and expensive.

T F   8. The thickness control on a slicing machine should be set at zero when the machine is not in use.

T F   9. A Number 16 scoop holds about 2 oz (60 g) of food.

T **F**   10. Refrigerators operate best when they are as full as possible.

T F   11. Induction cook tops work best with heavy aluminum pots and pans.

T **F**   12. The temperature inside a wood-burning hearth oven is controlled by adjusting the size of the flame with the thermostat.

T F   13. An immersion blender can be used to purée a sauce directly in the sauce pot.

T F   14. A sauteuse has sloping sides and a sautoire has straight sides.

Chapter 4

Basic Principles of Cooking and Food Science

This chapter presents much of the basic cooking language that you will use nearly every day. It is important to learn these terms well so that you can communicate effectively as a professional.

After studying Chapter 4, you should be able to:

1. Name the most important components of foods and describe what happens to them when they are cooked.

2. Name and describe three ways in which heat is transferred to food in order to cook it.

3. Describe the two factors or changes in cooked foods that determine doneness.

4. List three factors that affect cooking times.

5. Explain the advantage of boiling or simmering in a covered pot. Describe three situations in which a pot should not be covered during simmering or boiling.

6. Explain how cooking temperature affects the doneness characteristics of a food item.

7. Explain the differences between moist-heat cooking methods, dry-heat cooking methods, and dry-heat cooking methods using fat.

8. Describe each basic cooking method used in the commercial kitchen.

9. Identify the five properties that determine the quality of a deep-fried product.

10. Describe the two main steps in the process of cooking sous vide.

11. List six safety guidelines for cooking sous vide.

12. Explain the difference between a seasoning and a flavoring ingredient and give examples of each.

13. Identify appropriate times for adding seasoning ingredients to the cooking process in order to achieve optimal results.

14. Identify appropriate times for adding flavoring ingredients to the cooking process in order to achieve optimal results.

15. List eleven guidelines for using herbs and spices in cooking.

A. Terms

Fill in each blank with the term that is defined or described.

Poach **1.** To cook very gently in a small quantity of water or other liquid that is hot but not actually bubbling.

blanch **2.** To partially cook by boiling.

braise **3.** To cook covered in a small amount of liquid, after first browning the item.

steam **4.** The transfer of heat by the movement of air, steam, or liquid.

Coagulation **5.** The firming and shrinking of proteins due to heat.

Sautée **6.** To cook quickly, uncovered, in a small amount of fat.

deep fry **7.** To cook submerged in hot fat.

papillote **8.** Wrapped in paper for cooking.

Caramelization **9.** The browning of sugars due to heat.

broil **10.** To cook with radiant heat from above.

herbs **11.** The leaves of certain plants used for seasoning.

Zest **12.** The colored outer portion of citrus peel.

13. To cook uncovered in a skillet or sauté pan without added fat.

14. To cook with dry heat created by the burning of hardwood or by the hot coals of hardwood.

Roast **15.** To cook large cuts of meat or poultry by surrounding them with hot, dry air.

16. Two types of radiation or radiant energy used for cooking.

Simmer **17.** To cook in water or other liquid that is bubbling gently.

18. The process by which starch granules absorb water and swell in size.

19. The transfer of heat directly from one item to another item touching it, or from one part of an item to another.

20. Cooking methods in which heat is transferred to food by water or steam.

21. The temperature at which fat begins to smoke and to break down rapidly.

Steaming **22.** To cook by direct contact with steam.

23. To swirl a liquid in a cooking pan to dissolve particles of food remaining on the bottom.

24. The taste perception of "meatiness"; sometimes called the fifth basic taste.

_____ 25. A mixture in which one substance, called the *dispersed phase*, is evenly distributed in another substance, called the *continuous phase*.

_____ 26. A mixture as described in question 25 in which the continuous phase is water.

_____ 27. To enhance the natural flavor of food by adding small quantities of ingredients such as salt.

_pan fry_____ 28. To cook in a moderate amount of fat in an uncovered pan.

_____ 29. To cook with dry heat in the presence of smoke, such as on a rack over wood chips in a covered pan.

_Sous vide_____ 30. French term for *under vacuum*.

_____ 31. The reaction, caused by heat, that results in browning of the surface of meat.

_____ 32. The term that describes a protein that has uncoiled due to heat.

_____ 33. The harmony of ingredient flavors and aromas that the cook creates by selecting and combining ingredients for a dish.

B. Deep-Frying Review

1. What important quality must a fat possess in order to be good for deep-frying? _____

_____

2. What is the normal range of temperatures for deep-frying most foods? _____

3. List six enemies of frying fat; for each, state one way to protect fat from it.

(1) _____

_____

(2) _____

_____

(3) _____

_____

(4) _____

_____

(5) _____

_____

(6) _____

_____

4. How long do deep-fried foods hold after being cooked, and what is the proper way to hold them? _____

_____

_____

5. Why should frying baskets not be overloaded? _____

_____

6. List four characteristics that indicate good quality in fried foods. _____

_____

_____

_____

C. Microwave Review

1. It is often said that microwaves cook foods from the inside out. Is this true, partly true, or false? Explain why.

_____

_____

_____

2. Microwave ovens are probably used more for heating up cooked foods than for cooking raw foods. If this is true, why are microwave ovens so often used in restaurants where food is prepared to order?

_____

_____

_____

3. How well do microwaves go through aluminum foil? _____

_____

4. Why is accurate timing important when using a microwave oven? _____

_____

5. List three ways to help make sure that foods heat or cook evenly in a microwave oven. _____

_____

_____

_____

6. True or false: Dry foods heat more quickly in a microwave oven than moist ones do. Explain why or why not.

_____

_____

_____

D. Sous Vide Review

1. Briefly describe how tender meats and poultry are usually cooked in the sous vide process. Include temperatures and times. _____

_____

_____

_____

2. Briefly describe how tough meats are usually cooked in the sous vide process. Include temperatures and times.

_____

_____

_____

3. Briefly describe how a fish fillet might be cooked in the sous vide process. Include temperatures and times.

_____

_____

_____

4. Why is sous vide cooking useful for preparing artichokes? _____

_____

5. What categories of bacteria can be a hazard in sous vide cooking? Why? _____

_____

_____

6. After cooking, foods in vacuum packs should immediately be _____

or _____

7. What piece of equipment is most often used for precise temperature control when cooking sous vide items in a

water bath? _____

E. Herb and Spice Reference

It is important to become familiar with the appearance, aroma, and flavor of herbs and spices. Spice charts that describe flavors can be helpful, but there is no substitute for your own experience. Since everyone perceives flavors and aromas differently, a chart that describes herbs and spices in your own words can be your most helpful reference.

This chart may be completed on your own or as assigned by your instructor. Examine each herb or spice just as it is when it comes from its container. Fill in each space by describing your own impressions of its appearance (color and shape), smell, and taste. (The first column can be used to check off those spices assigned by your instructor.) The spaces at the end can be used for additional items not on the list.

√ Product	Appearance	Aroma	Taste
_____ Allspice			
_____ Anise seed			
_____ Basil			
_____ Bay leaf			
_____ Caraway seed			
_____ Cardamom, whole			
_____ Cardamom, ground			
_____ Cayenne or red pepper			

√	Product	Appearance	Aroma	Taste
_____	Celery seed, whole			
_____	Celery salt			
_____	Chili powder			
_____	Cilantro			
_____	Cinnamon, ground			
_____	Cinnamon stick			
_____	Cloves, ground			
_____	Cloves, whole			
_____	Coriander seed, whole			
_____	Cumin seed, whole			
_____	Cumin seed, ground			
_____	Curry powder			
_____	Fennel seed			
_____	Ginger, ground			
_____	Mace, ground			
_____	Marjoram			
_____	Nutmeg, ground			

√	Product	Appearance	Aroma	Taste
_____	Oregano			
_____	Paprika, Hungarian			
_____	Paprika, Spanish			
_____	Pepper, black			
_____	Pepper, white			
_____	Rosemary			
_____	Sage			
_____	Sichuan peppercorns			
_____	Star anise			
_____	Tarragon			
_____	Thyme			

Chapter 5

Menus, Recipes, and Cost Management

Chapter 5 introduces you to two of the most important documents in food service: the menu and the recipe. First, you are introduced to some of the basic concepts in menu planning. Then you become acquainted with the structure and functions of written recipes.

In order to use these documents to manage the operations of a kitchen, you learn the basic elements of kitchen math. In particular, you learn about the following:

1. Handling units of measure.
2. Converting recipe yields.
3. Making food cost calculations.
   (a) Working with food cost percentages.
   (b) Performing yield tests.
   (c) Calculating portion costs.

Exercises to give you practice with these important calculations are included here. Later chapters contain additional exercises to help you develop these essential skills.

After studying Chapter 5, you should be able to:

1. Explain how the makeup of a menu depends on the type of meal and on the institution using it.
2. Describe the differences between static and cycle menus, and between à la carte and table d'hôte menus.
3. List in order of their usual service the courses that might appear on modern menus.
4. Devise balanced menus that contain an adequate variety of foods and that can be efficiently and economically prepared.
5. Describe the problems and limitations of written recipes and the importance of using judgment when cooking.

6. **Discuss the structure and functions of standardized recipes.**

7. **Use and understand the recipes in this book to practice basic cooking techniques.**

8. **Measure ingredients and portions.**

9. **Use metric measurements.**

10. **Convert recipes to higher or lower yields.**

11. **Perform yield-cost analysis.**

12. **Calculate raw food costs.**

A. Terms

Fill in each blank with the term that is defined or described.

_____ 1. A menu on which each individual item is listed separately with its own price.

_____ 2. A food or group of foods served at one time or intended to be eaten at one time.

_____ 3. A menu that offers the same dishes every day.

_____ 4. A menu on which one price for the entire meal is given, and customers may choose dishes for each course offered.

_____ 5. A menu on which prices are listed for complete meals rather than for each separate item; prices vary depending on the meal the customer chooses.

_____ 6. A menu that changes every day for a certain period, after which the daily menus are repeated in the same order.

_____ 7. A menu that offers many courses of small portions, intended to showcase the chef's specialties.

_____ 8. A set of instructions describing the way a particular establishment prepares a particular dish.

_____ 9. A prefix in the metric system meaning "one thousand" (1000).

_____ 10. The basic unit of weight in the metric system, equal to about $\frac{1}{30}$ of an ounce.

_____ 11. The weight of a food item as purchased, before any trimming is done.

_____ 12. The basic unit of volume in the metric system, equal to approximately one quart.

_____ 13. A prefix in the metric system meaning "one one-thousandth" ($\frac{1}{1000}$).

_____ **14.** The raw food cost or portion cost of a menu item divided by the menu price (expressed as a percent).

_____ **15.** The basic unit of length in the metric system, equal to a little more than a yard.

_____ **16.** The basic unit of temperature in the metric system.

_____ **17.** A prefix in the metric system meaning "one tenth" ($\frac{1}{10}$).

_____ **18.** The weight of a raw food item after all nonedible or all nonservable parts have been trimmed off.

_____ **19.** The weight of a food item as served.

_____ **20.** A prefix in the metric system meaning "one one-hundredth" ($\frac{1}{100}$).

_____ **21.** The total cost of all the ingredients in a recipe, divided by the number of portions served.

B. Menu Review

1. List three types of establishments likely to have a cycle menu: _____,

_____, _____; and two

types likely to have a static menu: _____, _____.

2. Suppose you are planning a lunch menu for a small cafe in the heart of a business district where there are many offices and shops. What are three factors that will affect the kinds of foods you will include on the menu? Briefly explain each factor.

_____

_____

_____

_____

_____

_____

3. Three characteristics of foods—flavor, texture, and appearance—should be considered in order to build a menu with variety and balance (see pages 98-99 in the textbook). For each of these factors, list *three pairs* of foods that you would serve together. Try not to use any of the examples in the text. (An example is given to get you started.)

Texture Balance:

Example: breaded, fried chicken breast (crisp breading) with buttered spinach (soft).

(a) _____

_____

(b) _____

_____

(c) _____

_____

Flavor Balance:

(a) _____

_____

(b) _____

_____

(c) _____

_____

Appearance (including color and shape) Balance:

(a) _____

_____

(b) _____

_____

(c) _____

_____

4. From the point of view of "truth in menu," what do the following terms mean?

(a) homemade: _____

_____

(b) fresh: _____

_____

(c) imported: _____

_____

(d) jumbo shrimp: _____

_____

5. List the following courses in the order in which they would be served in a formal dinner: roast rack of lamb with spring vegetables; jellied consommé; poached fillet of sole with white wine sauce; caviar; apple tart.

_____

_____

_____

_____

_____

6. The following menus are missing one or more dishes or courses. Based on what you have learned about menu balance, fill in the blanks with your own suggestions.

(a) Tomato soup

   Roast prime ribs of beef

      Baked potato

      Vegetable: _____

(b) Cream of mushroom soup

   Mixed green salad

   Grilled lamb chops

      Vegetable: _____

      Starch: _____

(c) Shrimp cocktail

Vegetable beef soup

Main course: _____

    side dish(es): _____

    _____

(d) Appetizer: _____

Mixed green salad

Batter-fried shrimp

    Rice pilaf

    Vegetable: _____

(e) First course: _____

Grilled salmon steak with dill butter

    Steamed rice

    Vegetable: _____

(f) Soup: _____

Fried chicken

    Biscuits

    Corn

(g) Smoked salmon canapés

Beef consommé

Main course: _____

    Buttered asparagus

    Whipped potatoes

(h) Vegetable soup

Roast pork loin with garlic and sage

    Vegetable: _____

    Starch: _____

(i) Luncheon special: macaroni and cheese

    Any other course or side dish:

    _____

(j) Luncheon special: hot roast beef sandwich, potato chips

    Any other course or side dish:

    _____

C. Units of Measure

Fill in the blanks by making the correct conversions. For example:

6 tbsp = __3__ fl oz
18 oz = __1__ lb __2__ oz
32 oz = __2__ lb __0__ oz

1. 2¼ lb = _____ oz

2. ½ cup = _____ fl oz

3. 57 oz = _____ lb _____ oz

4. 36 fl oz = _____ pt _____ fl oz

5. 7¾ qt = _____ fl oz

6. 15 tsp = _____ tbsp

7. 22 oz = _____ lb _____ oz

8. 256 fl oz = _____ gal

9. 12 qt = _____ gal

10. 8 lb 8 oz = _____ oz

11. 3¾ lb = _____ lb _____ oz

12. 9 cups = _____ pt

13. 44 oz   = _____ lb _____ oz

14. 16 cups = _____ qt

15. ¾ qt   = _____ fl oz

16. 2.6 kg = _____ g

17. 3.5 L   = _____ mL

18. 6 dL   = _____ L

19. 1250 g = _____ kg

20. 22 cm   = _____ mm

21. .55 kg = _____ g

22. 6500 g = _____ kg

23. 750 dL = _____ L

24. 5 cL   = _____ dL

25. 4.6 kg = _____ g

26. 550 g   = _____ kg

27. 750 mL = _____ L

28. 50 mm   = _____ cm

29. 1.225 kg = _____ g

30. 0.6 L   = _____ mL

D. Recipe Conversion

The following ingredients and quantities are for gazpacho, a cold vegetable soup. The recipe yields 12 portions at 6 oz each. Convert the recipe to the yields indicated.

	12 portions, 6 oz each	30 portions, 6 oz each	36 portions, 8 oz each
Tomatoes	2½ lb	_____	_____
Cucumbers	1 lb	_____	_____
Onions	8 oz	_____	_____
Green peppers	4 oz	_____	_____
Crushed garlic	½ tsp	_____	_____
Bread crumbs, fresh	2 oz	_____	_____
Cold water or tomato juice	1 pt	_____	_____
Red wine vinegar	3 fl oz	_____	_____
Olive oil	5 fl oz	_____	_____
Salt	to taste	_____	_____
Pepper	to taste	_____	_____
Lemon juice	3 tbsp	_____	_____

Recipe Conversion—Metric

The following ingredients and quantities are for gazpacho, a cold vegetable soup. The recipe yields 12 portions at 200 mL each. Convert the recipe to the yields indicated.

	12 portions, 200 mL each	30 portions, 200 mL each	36 portions, 250 mL each
Tomatoes	1250 g	_____	_____
Cucumbers	500 g	_____	_____
Onions	300 g	_____	_____
Green peppers	125 g	_____	_____
Crushed garlic	2 mL	_____	_____
Bread crumbs, fresh	60 g	_____	_____
Cold water or tomato juice	600 mL	_____	_____
Red wine vinegar	100 mL	_____	_____
Olive oil	150 mL	_____	_____
Salt	to taste	_____	_____
Pepper	to taste	_____	_____
Lemon juice	50 mL	_____	_____

E. Food Cost Percentages

For each of the following six problems, use the two figures that are given to calculate the third figure, and fill in the blank.

Food cost percentage	Portion cost	Menu price
1. 25%	_____	$ 6.00
2. _____	$2.50	$10.00
3. 30%	$3.60	_____
4. _____	$5.12	$12.95
5. 35%	$6.48	_____
6. 28%	_____	$ 7.50

F. Portion Cost

Cost out the following recipe. For prices of the ingredients, use figures supplied by your instructor or the *Sample Prices* in the Appendix of this *Study Guide*.

ITEM: **STUFFED BAKED POTATOES**

Ingredient	Recipe Quantity	AP Quantity	Price	Total Amount
Baking potatoes, 8 oz each	40	_____	_____	_____
Butter	12 oz	_____	_____	_____
Milk	1 pt	_____	_____	_____
Dry bread crumbs	2 oz	_____	_____	_____
Parmesan cheese	2 oz	_____	_____	_____

Total cost _____

Number of portions 40

Cost per portion _____

Portion Cost—Metric

Cost out the following recipe. For prices of the ingredients, use figures supplied by your instructor or the *Sample Prices* in the Appendix of this *Study Guide*.

ITEM: **STUFFED BAKED POTATOES**

Ingredient	Recipe Quantity	AP Quantity	Price	Total Amount
Baking potatoes, 225 g each	40	_____	_____	_____
Butter	350 g	_____	_____	_____
Milk	500 mL	_____	_____	_____
Dry bread crumbs	50 g	_____	_____	_____
Parmesan cheese	50 g	_____	_____	_____

Total cost _____

Number of portions   40

Cost per portion _____

G. Triming Loss

The exercises below are of two kinds, calculating yields and calculating amount needed. To do the calculations, you need to know the percentage yield for each vegetable or fruit, as listed in Chapters 16 and 21 of the text. For your convenience, the necessary percentages are repeated here.

Asparagus	55%
Apricots	94%
Bananas	70%
Broccoli	70%
Celery	75%
Cherries	82%
Figs	95%
Kiwi fruit	80%
Leeks	50%
Mangoes	75%
Okra	82%
Papayas	65%
Pineapple	50%
Potatoes	80%
Watermelon	45%
Zucchini	90%

Calculating Amount Needed

Assume you need the following quantities, EP, of the indicated fresh vegetables and fruits. Calculate the AP weight you need to get the required yield. Questions 1–10 use U.S. measures; questions 11–20 use metric measures. Answer whichever questions are assigned by your instructor. (When you have fractions of an ounce in your answer, round your answer to the next higher whole number. For example, if your answer is 13.46 ounces, round up to 14 ounces.)

	EP Weight Desired	AP Weight Needed
1. Asparagus	1 lb 4 oz	_____
2. Bananas	1½ lb	_____
3. Broccoli	5 lb	_____
4. Cherries	1 lb	_____
5. Celery	3 lb	_____
6. Figs	12 oz	_____
7. Leeks	1 lb	_____
8. Mangoes	2½ lb	_____
9. Papaya	6 oz	_____
10. Zucchini	3 lb	_____

	EP Weight Desired	AP Weight Needed
11. Asparagus	600 g	_____
12. Bananas	750 g	_____
13. Broccoli	2.5 kg	_____
14. Cherries	450 g	_____
15. Celery	1.5 kg	_____
16. Figs	350 g	_____
17. Leeks	450 g	_____
18. Mangoes	1.25 kg	_____
19. Papaya	180 g	_____
20. Zucchini	1.5 k	_____

Calculating Yield

Assume you have the following quantities, AP, of the indicated fresh vegetables and fruits. Calculate the EP weight you will have left after trimming. Questions 21–30 use U.S. measures; questions 31–40 use metric measures. Answer whichever questions are assigned by your instructor. (When you have fractions of an ounce in your answer, round your answer down to the next lower whole number. For example, if your answer is 13.46 ounces, round down to 13 ounces.)

	AP Weight	EP Weight
21. Apricots	2 lb	_____
22. Broccoli	3 lb	_____
23. Kiwi fruit	1½ lb	_____
24. Leeks	1 lb	_____
25. Okra	1 lb 4 oz	_____
26. Papaya	3 lb	_____
27. Pineapple	5 lb	_____
28. Potatoes	8 lb	_____
29. Watermelon	12 lb	_____
30. Zucchini	1 lb 12 oz	_____

	AP Weight	EP Weight
31. Apricots	1 kg	_____
32. Broccoli	1.5 kg	_____
33. Kiwi fruit	750 g	_____
34. Leeks	450 g	_____
35. Okra	600 g	_____
36. Papaya	1.5 kg	_____
37. Pineapple	2.5 kg	_____
38. Potatoes	4 kg	_____
39. Watermelon	6 kg	_____
40. Zucchini	850 g	_____

H. Raw Yield Test

Fill in the blanks in the following Yield Test form.

ITEM: **VEAL LEG TO SCALOPPINE**

AP weight: 34 lb   Price per lb: $5.50   Total cost: $187.00

Trim, Salvage, and Waste:

Item	Weight	Value/lb	Total value (lb × value/lb)
Fat	2 lb 12 oz	$ .05	_____
Bone	3 lb 12 oz	.30	_____
Ground veal	2 lb 8 oz	$5.29	_____
Stew meat	3 lb	$5.79	_____
Unusable trim	15 oz	0	_____
Cutting loss	_____	0	_____

Total weight of
trim, salvage,
and waste: _____

Total value of
trim, salvage,
and waste: _____

Total yield of
item (scaloppine):   20 lb 12 oz

Net cost of item: _____

Cost per lb: _____

Percentage of
increase: _____

Raw Yield Test—Metric

Fill in the blanks in the following Yield Test form.

ITEM: **VEAL LEG TO SCALOPPINE**

AP weight: 15 kg   Price per lb: $12.00   Total cost: $180.00

Trim, Salvage, and Waste:

Item	Weight	Value/kg	Total value (kg × value/kg)
Fat	1.25 kg	$ .10	_____
Bone	1.7 kg	.65	_____
Ground veal	1.2 kg	$11.49	_____
Stew meat	1.4 kg	$12.79	_____
Unusable trim	400 g	0	_____
Cutting loss	_____	0	_____

Total weight of
trim, salvage,
and waste: _____

Total value of
trim, salvage,
and waste: _____

Total yield of
item (scaloppine):   5.95 kg

Net cost of item: _____

Cost per kg: _____

Percentage of
increase: _____

Chapter 6

Nutrition

Chapter 6 is an introduction to the challenging and often changing study of nutrition. Here you will become familiar with many of the key terms and concepts of this science so that you can better understand how to plan and prepare nutritious, healthful meals and meal choices for your customers or clients.

After studying Chapter 6, you should be able to:

1. List and describe the six categories of nutrients, explain their functions in the body, and name some food sources of each.
2. Define the term *calorie* and describe the relationship between calories and weight gain.
3. List and describe the eight guidelines for maintaining a healthful diet.
4. Describe ways that cooks can incorporate nutrition principles into their cooking and their menu construction.

A. Terms

Fill in each blank with the term that is defined or described.

_____ 1. A food that provides few nutrients per calorie.

_____ 2. A measure of the relative quantity of nutrients per calorie in a food.

_____ 3. The amount of heat needed to raise the temperature of 1 kilogram of water by 1°C.

_____ 4. A food protein that contains all essential amino acids.

___deficiency___ 5. Any disease that is caused by the lack of a particular vitamin.

_____ 6. A component of some foods that cannot be digested or used by the body but that is important for the proper functioning of the intestinal tract.

_____Carbohydrate_____ **7.** A group of nutrients that includes starches and sugars.

_____ **8.** Two categories of fat that are liquid at room temperature.

_____

_____ **9.** A category of fat that is solid at room temperature.

_____ **10.** Of the three categories of fats listed in numbers 8 and 9, this one is considered the most healthful.

_____ **11.** Minerals that must be consumed in relatively large amounts in order to maintain body health.

_____ **12.** A type of fat that is required by the body but that must be eaten because it can't be produced by the body.

_____ **13.** A toxin produced when the body burns fat without the presence of carbohydrates.

_____ **14.** A class of fiber found inside plant cells. When eaten, it absorbs water and forms a kind of gel.

_____ **15.** A type of saturated fat that is rarely found in nature and that is usually manufactured by food companies. It is considered especially unhealthful.

_____ **16.** Combinations of fat and protein that carry fat and cholesterol through the blood stream.

_____ **17.** One of the compounds described in number 16, which helps remove cholesterol from the blood and eliminate it from the body.

_____ **18.** Two or more foods that, when eaten together, supply all the amino acids.

B. Short-Answer Questions

1. One ounce is equal to 28.35 grams. Therefore, how many calories are supplied by 1 ounce of sugar?

_____

1 ounce of starch: _____

1 ounce of fat: _____

1 ounce of protein: _____

How many calories are supplied by 25 grams of sugar?

_____

25 grams of starch: _____

25 grams of fat: _____

25 grams of protein: _____

2. For each of the following nutrients, list three major food sources:

protein: _____

_____

_____

fat: _____

_____

_____

carbohydrate: _____

_____

_____

Vitamin C: _____

_____

_____

Vitamin A: _____

_____

_____

3. What is the most important function of carbohydrates in the body? _____

_____

4. What is the most important function of proteins in the body? _____

_____

5. Why is it important to include the B vitamins and vitamin C in the diet every day? _____

_____

6. What is the body's major source of the mineral sodium? _____

Why do health experts caution us to cut back on sodium in the diet? _____

_____

7. Give three specific examples of how you, as a restaurant chef, could reduce the fat content of foods that you prepare for your customers. _____

_____

_____

_____

_____

_____

8. How can using the freshest, highest quality ingredients help you cook more healthful meals? _____

_____

_____

_____

9. Explain the meaning of the term *empty calories.*

_____

_____

_____

10. List the five primary categories of foods as described in the USDA food pyramid. How many daily servings of each category of food is recommended for a 2000 calorie-per-day diet?

_____

_____

_____

_____

_____

11. List four types of foods that are considered to have the highest nutrient density.

_____

_____

_____

_____

12. Complete the following sentence: Considering the relationship between calorie intake, physical activity, and weight loss, the only way to lose weight is to _____ _____ .

13. Why are trans fats considered bad for health? _____

_____

_____

Chapter 7

Mise en Place

Well-planned preproduction is one of the most important elements of food service. It is essential for efficient production and service. Be sure you know this material well. In addition, be sure to practice the knife-handling techniques introduced in Chapter 7.

After studying Chapter 7, you should be able to:

1. Define *mise en place* and explain why care must be taken in its planning.
2. Describe five general steps used in planning mise en place.
3. Explain the difference in preparation requirements for set meal service and extended meal service.
4. List five guidelines to observe when sharpening a chef's knife.
5. Demonstrate major cutting techniques required in food preparation.
6. Describe basic precooking and marinating procedures.
7. Set up and use a standard breading station.
8. Define *convenience foods* in the context of mise en place and list eight guidelines for their use.

A. Terms

Fill in each blank with the term that is defined or described.

_____Julianne_____ 1. Cut into small, thin strips, about ⅛ × ⅛ × 1–2 in. (3 mm × 3 mm × 25–50 mm).

_____ 2. Any food that has been partially or completely prepared or processed by the manufacturer.

_____ 3. Cut into very fine dice, about ⅛ in. (3 mm) square.

Mise en place _____ **4.** French term for pre-preparation, meaning _put in place_.

_____ **5.** A semiliquid mixture containing flour or other starch, often used to coat items to be deep fried.

_____ **6.** To cut into very thin slices.

_____ **7.** To chop into very fine pieces.

_____ **8.** To soak a food in a seasoned liquid.

_____ **9.** To cut into thin but irregular strips, either with a knife or with a coarse grater.

_____ **10.** Cut into sticks, about ¼ × ¼ × 2–2½ in. (6 mm × 6 mm × 5–6 cm).

_____ **11.** To chop coarsely.

_____ **12.** Service of a meal at which all the customers eat at one time.

_____ **13.** Service of a meal at which customers eat at different times.

_____ **14.** The preliminary processing of ingredients to the point at which they can be used in cooking.

_____ **15.** A pre-preparation technique in which an item is cooked partially and very briefly in boiling water or hot fat.

_____ **16.** The measurement of portions to ensure that the correct amount of an item is served.

_____ **17.** The basic method used to apply crumb coatings to foods before frying or sautéing.

_____ **18.** Leafy vegetables cut into thin strips or shreds.

_____ **19.** The flavorful, colored outer part of a citrus peel.

_____ **20.** Thin cuts that are square or roughly square.

_____ **21.** A diamond-shaped cut.

_____ **22.** To cut into a barrel or oval shape.

_____ **23.** Two cuts made with a ball cutter.

_____

_____ **24.** A kind of marinade consisting primarily of salt and water, sometimes with added flavorings and/or sugar; usually used for meats and poultry.

B. True/False

T   F   **1.** One disadvantage of traditional large-batch cooking for set meal service is that hot foods deteriorate in quality when they are held at serving temperature.

T   F   **2.** For all recipes, final cooking must be started just before serving (when the waiter calls for the order) in order to produce the best quality foods.

T   F   **3.** When foods are cooked to order, the cooks don't need to begin work until the first orders come in.

T   F   **4.** A disadvantage of small-batch cooking is that it produces many leftovers.

T   F   **5.** When sharpening a knife on a stone, it is important to press down firmly on the blade.

T   F   **6.** The blade of the knife should be held at a 45-degree angle to the sharpening stone.

T   F   **7.** Most foods hold their quality better in the refrigerator than in the steam table.

T   F   **8.** After sharpening a knife with a steel, you should finish off the job with a few strokes on the stone to true the edge.

T   F   **9.** The tip of the chef's knife is used for cutting small items and for delicate work, because the blade is thinnest at the tip.

T   F   **10.** Whole spices, such as cloves and peppercorns, are more suitable for long marinations than for short ones.

T   F   **11.** Eggs are always used in batters for deep-frying.

T   F   **12.** Of the various types of marinades, dry marinades have the most tenderizing power.

C. Breading

In the space below, draw a diagram of a breading station.

Chapter 8

Stocks and Sauces

This is not only the first production chapter in the text, but it is also one of the most important. The techniques used in the making of stocks and sauces are the foundation of much of the work that is done in the commercial kitchen. Please study and review this material well.

After studying Chapter 8, you should be able to:

1. Prepare basic mirepoix.

2. Flavor liquids using a sachet d'épices, or spice bag.

3. Prepare white veal or beef stocks, chicken stock, fish stock, and brown stock.

4. Cool and store stocks correctly.

5. Prepare meat, chicken, and fish glazes.

6. Evaluate the quality of convenience bases, and use convenience bases.

7. Explain the functions of sauces, and list five qualities that a sauce adds to foods.

8. Prepare white, blonde, and brown roux, and use them to thicken liquids.

9. Prepare and use *beurre manié*.

10. Thicken liquids with cornstarch and other starches.

11. Prepare and use egg yolk and cream liaison.

12. Finish a sauce with raw butter (*monter au beurre*).

13. Prepare the five leading sauces: béchamel, velouté, brown sauce or espagnole, tomato, and hollandaise.

14. Prepare small sauces from leading sauces.

15. Identify and prepare five simple butter sauces.

16. Prepare compound butters and list their uses.

17. Prepare pan gravies.

18. Prepare miscellaneous hot and cold sauces.

A. Terms

Fill in each blank with the term that is defined or described.

_____ 1. Clear, thin liquid flavored by soluble substances extracted from meat, poultry, fish, and their bones, and from vegetables and seasonings.

_____ 2. Cheesecloth bag containing spices and herbs, used to flavor liquids.

_____ 3. Flavorful liquid, usually thickened, used to season, flavor, and enhance other foods.

_____ 4. Stock that is reduced until it coats the back of a spoon.

_____ 5. The process of boiling or simmering a liquid to evaporate part of the water.

_____ 6. The uniform mixture of two unmixable substances, usually two liquids.

_____ 7. Mixture of raw butter and various flavoring ingredients.

_____ 8. Basic sauce used in the production of other sauces.

_____ 9. Finished sauce, consisting of one of the basic sauces plus flavorings and other finishing ingredients.

_____ 10. Basic sauce consisting of thickened white stock.

_____ 11. Basic sauce consisting primarily of cooked, thickened milk.

_____ 12. Mixture of rough-cut or diced vegetables (usually including onion, celery, and carrot), and sometimes herbs and spices; this mixture is used for flavoring.

_____ 13. Combination of fresh herbs, tied together, used for flavoring.

_____ 14. Substance, extracted from connective tissue during stock making, which gives body to stock and which causes good stock to thicken or solidify when chilled.

_____ 15. The process of raising a stock pot onto blocks in a cold-water bath, so that the cold water can circulate better and cool the stock more quickly.

_____ 16. Unthickened juices from a roast, seasoned and served with the roast.

_____ 17. Term used on menus to describe meats served with the juices described in number 16.

_____ 18. Cooked mixture of equal parts flour and butter, used to thicken liquids.

_____ 19. Uncooked mixture of equal parts flour and raw butter, used to thicken liquids.

_____ 20. Brown stock that has been reduced until it is thick enough to coat the back of a spoon.

_____ 21. Chicken stock that has been reduced until it is thick enough to coat the back of a spoon.

_____ 22. Mixture of cold water and starch, such as cornstarch, used to thicken a liquid.

_____ 23. Half onion, burnt on a flattop or in a heavy skillet; used to add color to stock.

_____ 24. Onion pierced with a whole clove and bay leaf; used to flavor sauces and other simmered liquids.

_____ 25. Mixture of cream and egg yolks, used to thicken and enrich a sauce or soup.

_____ 26. Type of starch, used to thicken liquids, that keeps its binding or thickening power even after having been frozen.

_____ 27. Term meaning *until dry,* used in connection with the term defined in number 5.

_____ 28. Mixture of half brown sauce and half brown stock, reduced by half.

_____ 29. To swirl liquid in a pan to dissolve cooked particles of food remaining on the bottom.

_____ 30. To finish a sauce by swirling in a little raw butter until it melts and blends in.

_____ 31. Sauce made by thickening brown stock with cornstarch or similar starch.

_____ 32. Sauce made with the juices or drippings of the meat or poultry with which it is served.

_____ 33. Butter that is heated until it turns light brown.

_____ 34. Purified butterfat made by melting raw butter and removing the water and milk solids.

_____ 35. Sauce made by whipping a large amount of butter into a small amount of a flavorful reduction.

_____ 36. Purée of vegetables or fruits, used as a sauce.

_____ 37. Caramelized sugar dissolved in vinegar, used to flavor sauces.

_____ 38. Sauce consisting of a mixture of raw or cooked chopped vegetables, herbs, and occasionally fruits and frequently chiles.

_____ 39. Sauce based on the pan juices released during the cooking of a meat or other food. Pan gravy is one example of this type of sauce.

_____ 40. Mixture of chopped vegetables (and sometimes fruits), at least one of which has been pickled in vinegar or a salt solution.

_____ 41. Cooked fruit or vegetable condiment that is sweet, spicy, and tangy.

_____ 42. Sauce consisting of heavy cream that has been reduced until slightly thickened, blended with stock or other liquid and flavorings.

_____ 43. Term used to indicate the right coating texture for a sauce.

_____ 44. Stock made with bones that have already been used once in stock-making.

B. Stock-Making Review

Stock making is one of the most fundamental of all kitchen techniques, and you should be able, without hesitation, to describe in detail how to make it.

List the ingredients and the proper quantities to make 1 gal (or 4 L), first of white stock, then of brown stock. For each product, use the space after the ingredients to list the steps in production. It is not necessary to explain the steps, as the textbook does, but be sure to include all the steps, and number the steps to make the procedure easier to read.

White Stock

Ingredients: Quantities to make 1 gal (4 L)

Procedure:

Brown Stock

Ingredients: Quantities to make 1 gal (4 L)

Procedure:

C. Sauce Families I

To review the composition of the five Leading Sauces, fill in the names of the sauces, the liquid that forms the base of the sauce, and the thickening agent.

Leading Sauce	Liquid	Thickening Agent
_____	_____	_____
_____	_____	_____
_____	_____	_____
_____	_____	_____
_____	_____	_____

D. Sauce Families II

Review the composition of Small Sauces by completing the following chart. In the left column are listed a number of Small Sauces. For each one, list the Leading Sauce that it is based on, as well as the most important flavoring or finishing ingredient(s).

Small Sauce	Leading Sauce	Principal Flavoring
1. Mornay	_____	_____
2. Robert	_____	_____
3. Chasseur	_____	_____
4. Suprême	_____	_____
5. Madeira	_____	_____
6. Bercy (white)	_____	_____
7. Aurora	_____	_____
8. Bordelaise	_____	_____
9. Nantua	_____	_____
10. Mousseline	_____	_____
11. Foyot	_____	_____

12. Creole _____ _____

13. White Wine _____ _____

14. Allemande _____ _____

15. Cream _____ _____

16. Lyonnaise _____ _____

17. Mushroom (brown) _____ _____

18. Maltaise _____ _____

19. Hungarian _____ _____

20. Portugaise _____ _____

21. Diable _____ _____

22. Mustard _____ _____

23. Choron _____ _____

24. Bercy (brown) _____ _____

E. Béchamel Review

In the following space, explain how to make Béchamel Sauce. Be sure to include all the necessary steps, and number the steps to make the procedure easier to read. Include ingredient quantities if your instructor asks you to do so.

F. Hollandaise Review

In the following space, explain how to make Hollandaise Sauce. Be sure to include all necessary steps, and number the steps to make the procedure easier to read. Include ingredient quantities if your instructor asks you to do so.

G. Recipe Conversion

The following ingredients and quantities are for a barbecue sauce recipe that yields ½ gal. Convert the recipe to the yields indicated.

	½ gal	1½ gal	1 quart
Tomato purée	1 qt		
Water	1 pt		
Worcestershire sauce	⅔ cup		
Cider vinegar	½ cup		
Vegetable oil	½ cup		
Onion	8 oz		
Garlic, crushed	4 tsp		
Sugar	2 oz		
Dry mustard	1 tbsp		
Chili powder	2 tsp		
Black pepper	1 tsp		
Salt	to taste		

Recipe Conversion—Metric

The following ingredients and quantities are for a barbecue sauce recipe that yields 2 L. Convert the recipe to the yields indicated.

	2 liters	6 liters	1 liter
Tomato purée	1 L	_____	_____
Water	500 mL	_____	_____
Worcestershire sauce	175 mL	_____	_____
Cider vinegar	125 mL	_____	_____
Vegetable oil	125 mL	_____	_____
Onion	250 g	_____	_____
Garlic, crushed	20 mL	_____	_____
Sugar	60 g	_____	_____
Dry mustard	15 mL	_____	_____
Chili powder	10 mL	_____	_____
Black pepper	5 mL	_____	_____
Salt	to taste	_____	_____

H. Portion Cost

Cost out the following recipe. For prices of the ingredients, use figures supplied by your instructor or the *Sample Prices* in the Appendix of this *Study Guide*. For the sake of this exercise, assume that the quantities given for the vegetables are AP quantities (see pages 115 and 119 in the textbook).

ITEM: **SWEET AND SOUR SAUCE**

Yield: 1 qt

Ingredient	Recipe Quantity	AP Quantity	Price	Total Amount
Chicken stock	1 qt	_____	_____	_____
Cornstarch	1 oz	_____	_____	_____
Sugar	8 oz	_____	_____	_____
Soy sauce	2 oz	_____	_____	_____
Green bell pepper	2 oz	_____	_____	_____
Red bell pepper	2 oz	_____	_____	_____
Onion	4 oz	_____	_____	_____
Red wine vinegar	½ cup	_____	_____	_____
Ginger	½ tsp (¹⁄₂₅ oz)	_____	_____	_____
Salt	to taste	_____	_____	_____
Pepper	to taste	_____	_____	_____

Total cost _____

Number of 2-oz portions _____

Cost per portion _____

Portion Cost—Metric

Cost out the following recipe. For prices of the ingredients, use figures supplied by your instructor or the *Sample Prices* in the Appendix of this *Study Guide*. For the sake of this exercise, assume that the quantities given for the vegetables are AP quantities (see pages 115 and 119 in the textbook).

ITEM: **SWEET AND SOUR SAUCE**

Yield: 1 L

Ingredient	Recipe Quantity	AP Quantity	Price	Total Amount
Chicken stock	1 L	_____	_____	_____
Cornstarch	25 g	_____	_____	_____
Sugar	250 g	_____	_____	_____
Soy sauce	75 mL	_____	_____	_____
Green bell pepper	60 g	_____	_____	_____
Red bell pepper	60 g	_____	_____	_____
Onion	125 g	_____	_____	_____
Red wine vinegar	125 mL	_____	_____	_____
Ginger	2 mL (1 g)	_____	_____	_____
Salt	to taste	_____	_____	_____
Pepper	to taste	_____	_____	_____

Total cost _____

Number of
50-mL portions _____

Cost per portion _____

Chapter 9

Soups

The procedures for some kinds of soup are fairly easy to learn, so these are some of the first products that culinary students learn. On the other hand, some other soup-making procedures are much more difficult, and require more study and practice. But whether you are learning simple procedures or complicated ones, you must pay close attention to the proper techniques in order to make quality soups.

After studying Chapter 9, you should be able to:

1. Describe three basic categories of soups.
2. Identify standard appetizer and main course portion sizes for soups.
3. State the procedures for holding soups for service and for serving soups at the proper temperature.
4. Prepare clarified consommé.
5. Prepare vegetable soups and other clear soups.
6. Prepare cream soups.
7. Prepare purée soups.
8. Prepare bisques, chowders, specialty soups, and national soups.

A. Terms

Fill in each blank with the term that is defined or described.

_____ 1. A thickened cream soup made from shellfish.

_____ 2. A rich, flavorful stock or broth that has been clarified to make it clear and transparent.

_____ 3. The mixture of ingredients used to clarify a stock to make the product described in number 2.

_____   4. The mixture described in number 3, after it has coagulated and floated to the surface of the stock.

_____   5. A soup that is thickened by puréeing one or more of its ingredients.

_____   6. A clear, seasoned stock or broth with the addition of one or more vegetables and sometimes meat or poultry products or starches.

_____   7. A general French term for soup, often used to refer to a thick, hearty soup.

_____   8. A soup that is thickened with roux or other thickening agent and contains milk and/or cream.

_____   9. A cold soup made of puréed leeks and onions with cream.

_____   10. A clarified soup, as described in number 2, flavored strongly with tomato.

_____   11. A type of hearty American soup often containing seafood, potatoes, and milk.

_____   12. Another name for Purée of Carrot Soup.

_____   13. A specialty soup, from Russia, containing beets as a major ingredient.

_____   14. A flavorful liquid made by simmering meat and vegetables, often used as a soup.

B. Consommé Review

The procedure for clarifying consommé is one that you should know well. Using numbered steps, explain how to make consommé. Be sure to include all the necessary steps. Include ingredient quantities if your instructor asks you to do so.

C. True/False

T   F   **1.** Most vegetable soups should be cooked a long time so that the broth will develop flavor.

T   F   **2.** The four basic ingredients used to clarify a stock are ground meat, mirepoix, tomato product, and an acid ingredient.

T   F   **3.** When you are making chicken noodle soup, it is best to cook the noodles separately if you want to keep the broth clear.

T   F   **4.** Beef loin is the best meat to use for clarifying stock.

T   F   **5.** A typical appetizer-size portion of soup is 6 to 8 oz (175 to 250 mL).

T   F   **6.** The best way to maintain the quality of a large quantity of vegetable soup is to keep it hot in a steam table throughout the service period.

T   F   **7.** Protein coagulation is the process that makes possible the clarification of stock.

T   F   **8.** A well-made consommé has a rich, dark brown color.

T   F   **9.** Based on the production method, lobster bisque could be classified as a cream soup.

T   F   **10.** When it is being clarified, a consommé should be brought to a rapid boil so that the proteins will coagulate properly.

T   F   **11.** Consommé Printanière is garnished with various spring vegetables.

T   F   **12.** For best flavor, it is always best to include as many different vegetables as possible in a clear vegetable soup.

T   F   **13.** Starch thickeners help to stabilize milk and cream so that they are less likely to curdle.

T   F   **14.** Mirepoix for cream soups should be browned lightly to develop flavor.

T   F   **15.** A starchy product is usually one of the ingredients in a purée soup.

D. Cream Soup Review

Explain how to make Cream of Carrot Soup. Use either Method 1 or Method 2, or whichever method your instructor assigns. Write the procedure in the form of numbered steps. If your instructor asks you to do so, include ingredient quantities.

E. Recipe Conversion

The following ingredients and quantities are for a Potato Chowder recipe that yields 24 portions, 8 oz each. Convert the recipe to the yields indicated.

	24 portions, 8 oz each	36 portions, 8 oz each	24 portions, 6 oz each
Salt pork	8 oz	_____	_____
Onions	12 oz	_____	_____
Celery	3 oz	_____	_____
Flour	4 oz	_____	_____
Chicken stock	3½ qt	_____	_____
Potatoes	3 lb	_____	_____
Milk	3 pt	_____	_____
Heavy cream	1 cup	_____	_____
Chopped parsley	4 tbsp	_____	_____

Recipe Conversion—Metric

The following ingredients and quantities are for a Potato Chowder recipe that yields 24 portions, 250 mL each. Convert the recipe to the yields indicated.

	24 portions, 250 mL each	36 portions, 250 mL each	24 portions, 175 mL each
Salt pork	250 g	_____	_____
Onions	375 g	_____	_____
Celery	100 g	_____	_____
Flour	124 g	_____	_____
Chicken stock	3.5 L	_____	_____
Potatoes	1.5 kg	_____	_____
Milk	1.5 L	_____	_____
Heavy cream	250 mL	_____	_____
Chopped parsley	60 mL	_____	_____

F. Portion Cost

Cost out the following recipe. For prices of the ingredients, use figures supplied by your instructor or the *Sample Prices* in the Appendix of this *Study Guide*.

ITEM: **BORSCHT**

Ingredient	Recipe Quantity	AP Quantity	Price	Total Amount
Beef brisket	2 lb	_____	_____	_____
Beef stock	3½ qt	_____	_____	_____
Butter	4 oz	_____	_____	_____
Onion, EP*	8 oz	_____	_____	_____
Leeks, EP*	8 oz	_____	_____	_____
Cabbage, EP*	8 oz	_____	_____	_____
Beets	2 No. 2½ cans	_____	_____	_____
Tomato purée	4 oz	_____	_____	_____
Red wine vinegar	4 oz	_____	_____	_____
Sugar	1 oz	_____	_____	_____
Sour cream	12 oz	_____	_____	_____

Total cost _____

Number of portions   24

Cost per portion _____

Note: Remember that you need AP weights of all ingredients (see pages 115 and 119 in the textbook). Let's assume that you kept a record of the quantities needed when you made this recipe:

To get 8 oz EP onions, you needed 9 oz AP.

To get 8 oz EP leeks, you needed 1 lb AP.

To get 8 oz EP cabbage, you needed 10 oz AP.

Portion Cost—Metric

Cost out the following recipe. For prices of the ingredients, either use figures supplied by your instructor, or use the *Sample Prices* in the Appendix of this *Study Guide*.

ITEM: BORSCHT

Ingredient	Recipe Quantity	AP Quantity	Price	Total Amount
Beef brisket	1 kg	_____	_____	_____
Beef stock	3.5 L	_____	_____	_____
Butter	100 g	_____	_____	_____
Onion, EP*	250 g	_____	_____	_____
Leeks, EP*	250 g	_____	_____	_____
Cabbage, EP*	250 g	_____	_____	_____
Beets	2 No. 2½ cans	_____	_____	_____
Tomato purée	125 g	_____	_____	_____
Red wine vinegar	125 mL	_____	_____	_____
Sugar	25 g	_____	_____	_____
Sour cream	400 g	_____	_____	_____

Total cost _____

Number of portions   24

Cost per portion _____

Note: Remember that you need AP weights of all ingredients (see pages 115 and 119 in the textbook). Let's assume that you kept a record of the quantities needed when you made this recipe:

To get 250 g EP onions, you needed 275 g AP.

To get 250 g EP leeks, you needed 500 g AP.

To get 250 g EP cabbage, you needed 300 g AP.

Chapter 10

Understanding Meats and Game

Meats are such a large area of study that we have divided the subject matter into two chapters. This first chapter concentrates on basic product information. In particular, it discusses the general characteristics of the four most important meats—beef, lamb, veal, and pork. The great variety of meat cuts may be somewhat confusing at first, so careful review is called for.

After studying Chapter 10, you should be able to:

1. Describe the composition and structure of meat and explain how they relate to meat selection and cooking methods.

2. Explain the use of the federal meat inspection and grading system in selecting and purchasing meats.

3. Explain the effect that aging has on meat and identify the two primary aging methods.

4. Identify the primal cuts of beef, lamb, veal, and pork, and list the major fabricated cuts obtained from each of them.

5. Select appropriate cooking methods for the most important meat cuts, based on the meat's tenderness and other characteristics.

6. Prepare variety meats.

7. Identify the characteristics of game meats and select the appropriate cooking methods for them.

8. Determine doneness in cooked meats.

9. Store fresh meats and frozen meat to gain the maximum shelf life.

A. Terms

Fill in each blank with the term that is defined or described.

<u>Marbling</u>   **1.** In a piece of meat, the fat that is deposited within the muscle tissue.

<u>Collagen</u>   **2.** A type of connective tissue in meats that dissolves when cooked with moisture.

<u>Elastin</u>   **3.** A type of connective tissue that does not break down or dissolve when cooked.

Inspection **4.** A government procedure that checks the wholesomeness of meat, to make sure that it is fit to eat.

Grading **5.** A government procedure that checks the quality of meat.

Green Meat **6.** Meat that has not had enough time after slaughter to develop tenderness and flavor.

Primal cuts **7.** One of the primary divisions of meat quarters, foresaddles, hindsaddles, and carcasses as they are broken down into smaller cuts.

Carryover Cooking **8.** The continued rise of a roast's internal temperature after it has been removed from the oven.

medium rare **9.** The name given to the degree of doneness of a piece of meat that is cooked on the outside but still uncooked or barely cooked on the inside.

trichinosis **10.** A disease that could be transmitted by eating undercooked pork.

Institution Meat Purchase Specifications **11.** The four-word term that the letters IMPS stand for.

yield grading **12.** A grading system that indicates how much usable meat a carcass has in proportion to fat.

larding **13.** The process of inserting strips of fat into a piece of meat, usually a cut of meat that has little of its own fat.

Barding **14.** The process of tying sheets of fat over the surface of a cut of meat that does not have its own natural fat cover.

Variety Meats **15.** A group of meats consisting of organs, glands, and other meats that don't form part of the dressed carcass of the animal.

Sweetbreads **16.** The thymus gland of calves and other young animals, used as food.

tripe **17.** The muscular stomach lining of the beef animal, used as food.

Chitterlings **18.** Pork intestines, used as food.

Caul **19.** A fatty membrane covering a pig's stomach.

Venison **20.** Deer meat.

Boar **21.** Wild pig.

Hare **22.** An animal similar to rabbit but with dark red, gamy meat.

Irradiation **23.** The process of exposing foods to radiation in order to kill bacteria, parasites, and other potentially harmful organisms.

Dry-Aging **24.** The process of holding dressed carcasses of game animals or birds outside of refrigeration for a period before further cutting, processing, or cooking.

Silverskin **25.** Thin layer or membrane of connective tissue that often covers surface of a muscle.

B. Short-Answer Questions

Fill in the blanks to complete the following statements. You may need more than one word per blank.

1. The most accurate way to test the doneness of a roast is to _Use a meat thermometer_ .

2. As meat is aged, it gradually becomes tenderer. This is caused by _enzymes_ , which are naturally present in the meat.

3. _Veal_ is not aged because it doesn't have enough fat cover to protect it from drying out.

4. A meat is naturally tender if it comes from a _Older_ animal or if it comes from a muscle that had _more_ exercise.

5. Quality grading of meats _not_ (is/is not) required by law.

6. Some connective tissues can be broken down by heat, by acids, or by _tenderizers_ .

7. The top grade of beef is _Prime_ . The next two grades, in order, are _Choice_ and _Select_ .

8. The top three grades of veal, starting with the best, are _Prime_ , _Choice_ , and _good_ .

9. The top three grades of lamb, starting with the best, are _Prime_ , _Choice_ , and _good_ .

10. The first cut made to break down a carcass of lamb is located _between the 12th and 13th rib_ . This divides the carcass into two pieces called the _foresaddle_ and the _hindsaddle_ .

11. The first cut made to break down a carcass of beef is to divide it into two halves, called _sides_ , by cutting it _between rib 12 and thirteen into forequarter and hindquar_

12. The major bones in a primal rib of beef are _backbone, chime, and feather bones_ .

13. The bone that forms the stem of the T in a T-bone steak is called the _finger bones_ .

14. The major bones in a full loin of beef are _Ribs, backbone, chine, feather bone, finger bones_ .

15. The full loin of beef may be divided into two parts, called the _loin_ and the _Sirloin_ .

16. The standard full rack of lamb contains how many ribs? _13_

17. The major bones in a primal leg of veal are _backbone, tailbone, pelvic, rand bone, and hindshank_ .

18. Two examples of beef cuts that are almost always cooked by moist-heat methods are _Chuck_ and _Brisket_ .

19. Two examples of beef cuts that are almost always cooked by dry-heat methods are _rib_ and _Sirloin_ .

20. The usual method used to test the doneness of a steak being cooked on a grill is _touch_ .

21. Of the four types of kidneys discussed, _veal_ kidneys and _lamb_ kidneys are considered the most desirable.

22. The best way to cook tripe is by _blanching & simmering_ .

23. Tender cuts of venison, such as the loin, are best cooked to the rare stage because _it will dry out if cooked too long_

24. The common meat that bison or buffalo most resembles is _venison_ .

25. The most desirable parts of the rabbit carcass are the _forelegs_ and the _hindlegs_ .

C. Beef Primal Cuts

Cuts are identified by numbers in the following beef chart. In each of the numbered blanks after the chart, write the name of the cut corresponding to the number in the chart.

1. Chuck

2. Rib

3. Short loin

4. Full loin

5. Sirloin

6. round

7. flank

8. Short plate

9. Brisket

10. Shank

D. Pork Cuts

Cuts are identified by numbers in the following pork chart. In each of the numbered blanks after the chart, write the name of the cut corresponding to the number in the chart.

1. Jowl

2. boston butt

3. Fat back

4. loin

5. Ham

6. foot

7. spare ribs

8. bacon side (belly)

9. shoulder picnic

10. foot

E. The Round or Leg

Identify the various parts in the following diagram of a round steak, and fill in the numbered blanks with the names of the parts.

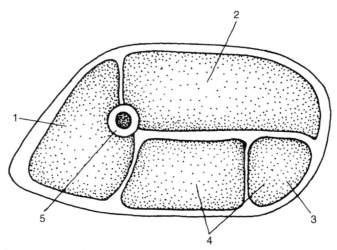

1. Knuckle or tip
2. Inside (top) round
3. eye round
4. Outside (bottom) round
5. leg or round bone

F. Fabricated Cuts

In the blank following the name of each cut, write the name of the primal cut from which it is taken.

1. Beef shoulder clod _____

2. Lamb rib chop _____

3. Beef sirloin steak _____

4. Veal loin chop _____

5. Beef rump _____

6. Canadian-style bacon _____

7. Boneless lamb rolled
   shoulder roast   _____

8. Corned beef brisket   _____

9. Beef porterhouse steak _____

10. Beef flank steak   _____

11. Pork rib chop   _____

12. Beef knuckle   _____

13. Beef hamburger   _____

14. Smoked daisy ham   _____

15. Bacon   _____

16. Leg of lamb roast   _____

17. Veal scaloppine   _____

18. Beef tenderloin steak _____

19. Beef short ribs   _____

20. Beef top round   _____

21. Smoked picnic ham   _____

22. Veal saddle roast   _____

23. Beef T-bone steak   _____

24. Beef strip loin steak _____

25. Lamb sirloin chop   _____

G. Raw Yield Test

Fill in the blanks in the following Yield Test form. (Instructions for completing this form are in Chapter 5 of the textbook, pages 109–110.)

ITEM: **BEEF STRIP LOIN (BONE IN) REGULAR TO TRIMMED STRIP LOIN STEAKS**

AP weight: 18 lb   Price per lb: $2.99   Total cost: $53.82

Trim, Salvage, and Waste:

Item	Weight	Value/lb	Total value (lb × value/lb)
Fat	2 lb 9 oz	$ .07	_____
Bone	4 lb 2 oz	.24	_____
Ground beef	11 oz	$2.39	_____
Cutting loss	_____	0	_____

Total weight of trim, salvage, and waste: _____   Total value of trim, salvage, and waste: _____

Total yield of item (steaks): 10 lb 8 oz

Net cost of item: _____

Cost per lb: _____

Percentage of increase: _____

Raw Yield Test—Metric

Fill in the blanks in the following Yield Test form. (Instructions for completing this form are in Chapter 5 of the textbook, pages 109–110, and in Appendix 4, page 1029.)

ITEM: **BEEF STRIP LOIN (BONE IN) REGULAR TO TRIMMED STRIP LOIN STEAKS**

AP weight: 8 kg   Price per kg: $6.79   Total cost: $54.32

Trim, Salvage, and Waste:

Item	Weight	Value/kg	Total value (kg × value/kg)
Fat	1.2 kg	$ .15	_____
Bone	1.9 kg	.55	_____
Ground beef	350 g	$5.25	_____
Cutting loss	_____	0	_____

Total weight of trim, salvage, and waste: _____

Total value of trim, salvage, and waste: _____

Total yield of item (steaks):   4.5 kg

Net cost of item: _____

Cost per kg: _____

Percentage of increase: _____

Chapter 11

Cooking Meats and Game

In this chapter, our examination shifts from product information to cooking techniques. The basic cooking methods, first discussed in Chapter 4, are applied to a range of meat types and cuts.

After studying Chapter 11, you should be able to:

1. Cook meats by roasting and baking.
2. Cook meats by broiling, grilling, and pan-broiling.
3. Cook meats by sautéing, pan-frying, and griddling.
4. Cook meats by simmering.
5. Cook meats by braising.
6. Cook variety meats.

A. Terms

Fill in each blank with the term that is defined or described.

_____ 1. Spooning fat drippings over a roast as it cooks.

_____ 2. To cook foods by surrounding them with hot, dry air.

_____ 3. Meat juice thickened with cornstarch or similar starch, served as a sauce with the meat.

_____ 4. A mixture of chopped parsley, bread crumbs, and garlic, used as a coating or topping for items such as roast rack of lamb.

_____   **5.** The process of stripping all the meat and fat off the ends of the rib bones on a roast, especially rack of lamb, for the sake of appearance.

_____   **6.** A German dish consisting of beef marinated and then cooked with vinegar and other ingredients.

_____   **7.** A brown lamb stew.

_____   **8.** To place meats on a grill or broiler in such a way that the hot bars of the grill make an attractive cross-hatching pattern on the meat.

_____   **9.** A broiled dish consisting of cubes of meat, usually lamb, and sometimes vegetables threaded on skewers.

_____   **10.** The muscular stomach lining of the beef animal, used as food.

_____   **11.** Thin, flattened slices of veal leg, usually cooked by sautéing.

_____   **12.** Flank steak or other cut of beef broiled rare and cut in thin slices.

_____   **13.** Beef round steaks braised in brown sauce.

_____   **14.** A small beef tenderloin steak cut about 1½ in. (4 cm) thick and weighing about 3 oz (90 g).

_____   **15.** A dish consisting of sautéed beef tenderloin tips in a sauce made with sour cream.

_____   **16.** To cook small pieces of meat by simmering or braising in a small amount of liquid that is then served with the meat as a sauce.

_____   **17.** A dish consisting of simmered corned beef and simmered vegetables, served together.

_____   **18.** A white stew of white meats cooked by simmering without preliminary browning, and served with a white sauce.

_____   **19.** A white stew made by cooking white meat in fat over low heat, without letting it brown, and then cooking in liquid.

_____   **20.** A common name for a large cut of meat, usually beef, cooked by braising.

_____   **21.** A classic French beef stew cooked in red wine and garnished with bacon pieces, mushrooms, and small onions.

_____   **22.** A Hungarian stew flavored with paprika.

_____   **23.** To swirl a liquid in a sauté pan or other pan to dissolve cooked particles of food remaining on the bottom.

_____   **24.** A North African spiced stew, traditionally cooked in an earthenware pot with a conical lid.

B. Roasting Review

The following statements consist of instructions and guidelines for roasting meats, but some key words are left out. Fill in the blanks to complete the sentences.

1. Select a roasting pan that has _____ sides; the size of the pan should be _____

    _____ .

2. When you are trimming the meat for a roast, heavy fat coverings should be _____

    _____ .

3. Unless it is a bone-in rib roast, the meat should be placed on a _____ .

4. The fat side of the meat should be _____ when it is placed in the pan.

5. If you are using a standard meat thermometer instead of an instant-read thermometer, position it in the meat

    so that the tip is _____ .

6. The oven should be _____ before the roast is put in.

7. If you are using a convection oven in place of a conventional oven, set the temperature _____ .

8. Most large roasts cook best at a _____ temperature.

9. Do not put a _____ on the pan, because this will trap _____ in the pan.
   Roasting is supposed to be a dry-heat cooking method.

10. The main purpose of using mirepoix when roasting meats is _____

    _____ .

11. Because of carry-over cooking, the meat should be removed from the oven _____ .

12. After the roast is removed from the oven, allow it to _____

    _____ .

13. If the cooked roast must be held in a warmer for a relatively long time, set the temperature _____

    _____ .

C. Braising Review

In one method for braising meats, the meat is cooked in a thickened sauce. Below are the steps for this procedure, but they are all out of order. Place the steps in the correct order by writing the number 1 in the blank before the first step, number 2 before the second step, and so on.

Caution: The steps may not all be written in the same way as in the text. In some cases, one step in the text may be divided into two steps here. In other cases, two steps might be combined into one step here. So think about the methods, and don't just copy the book.

_____ Add flour to make a roux.

_____ Adjust the seasonings and thickness of the sauce and skim off excess fat as necessary before serving.

_____ Heat a small amount of fat in the braising pan.

_____ Simmer with the cover on until the meat is tender.

_____ Collect all equipment and food supplies.

_____ Brown the roux.

_____ Put the meat in the pan and brown it well on all sides. Remove it from the pan.

_____ Return the meat to the pan.

_____ Stir in the stock and simmer until thickened.

_____ Add the mirepoix and brown it in the fat left in the pan.

_____ Add tomato product and sachet.

_____ Trim and prepare the meat for cooking as required.

In another method for braising meats, the meat is cooked in a flavorful stock instead of a thickened sauce, and braising liquid is made into a sauce after the meat is cooked. Below are the steps for this procedure, again out of order. Put them in the right order as in the above exercise.

_____ Skim the fat from the braising liquid. Make a roux and thicken the braising liquid with it to make a sauce.

_____ Add the mirepoix and brown it in the fat left in the pan.

_____ Strain and adjust the seasonings of the sauce.

_____ Collect all equipment and food supplies.

_____ Put the meat in the pan and brown it well on all sides. Remove it from the pan.

_____ Serve the meat with the sauce.

_____ Heat a small amount of fat in the braising pan.

_____ Put the meat back into the pan and add stock or other braising liquids, plus tomato product and sachet.

_____ Trim and prepare the meat for cooking as required.

_____ Take the cooked meat out of the braising liquid and keep the meat warm.

_____ Simmer with the cover on until the meat is tender.

D. True/False

T   F   **1.** If you are broiling two 1-inch-thick steaks, and one of them has been ordered well done while the other is to be rare, you should cook the well-done steak over higher heat.

T   F   **2.** Veal leg and veal shank are two good cuts to use for veal scaloppine.

T   F   **3.** Rack of lamb to be done rare should always be roasted at a low temperature.

T   F   **4.** Lamb shoulder is a suitable cut to be cooked by braising.

T   F   **5.** When sautéeing beef tenderloin tips, you should make sure the pan is hot before you add the meat.

T   F   **6.** Since oxtails are not naturally tender, they should be cooked by simmering or braising.

T   F   **7.** Salted and cured meats to be simmered are generally started in cold water.

T   F   **8.** A rule of thumb for broiling meats is "The shorter the cooking time, the higher the cooking temperature."

T   F   **9.** To sauté meats in the most efficient way, you should make sure that you use a small enough pan so that the meat covers the bottom completely.

T   F   **10.** Clarified butter should never be used for sautéing.

T   F   **11.** For some sautéed meat recipes, the pan that the meat was cooked in is deglazed to make a sauce for the meat.

T   F   **12.** When simmering corned beef, you should use enough cooking liquid to cover the meat by about one-third.

T   F   **13.** Stir-frying is similar to sautéing, except that in stir-frying, food items are mixed by flipping the pan, while in sautéing they are turned over with a spatula.

E. Recipe Conversion

The following ingredients and quantities are for a Roast Stuffed Lamb Shoulder recipe that yields 10 portions, 5 oz each. Convert the recipe to the yields indicated.

	10 portions, 5 oz each	30 portions, 5 oz each	75 portions, 4 oz each
Onion	4 oz	_____	_____
Garlic	1 tsp	_____	_____
Oil	2 oz	_____	_____
Bread crumbs, fresh	3 oz	_____	_____
Chopped parsley	⅓ cup	_____	_____
Rosemary	½ tsp	_____	_____
Black pepper	¼ tsp	_____	_____
Salt	½ tsp	_____	_____
Eggs, beaten	1	_____	_____
Boneless lamb shoulder	4 lb	_____	_____
Mirepoix	8 oz	_____	_____
Flour	2 oz	_____	_____
Brown stock	1 qt	_____	_____
Tomatoes, canned	4 oz	_____	_____

Recipe Conversion—Metric

The following ingredients and quantities are for a Roast Stuffed Lamb Shoulder recipe that yields 10 portions, 150 g each. Convert the recipe to the yields indicated.

	10 portions, 150 g each	30 portions, 150 g each	75 portions, 125 g each
Onion	125 g		
Garlic	5 mL		
Oil	50 mL		
Bread crumbs, fresh	100 g		
Chopped parsley	75 mL		
Rosemary	2 mL		
Black pepper	1 mL		
Salt	2 mL		
Eggs, beaten	1		
Boneless lamb shoulder	2 kg		
Mirepoix	250 g		
Flour	50 g		
Brown stock	1 L		
Tomatoes, canned	125 g		

F. Portion Cost

Cost out the following recipe. For prices of the ingredients, use figures supplied by your instructor or the *Sample Prices* in the Appendix of this *Study Guide*.

ITEM: **CHILE CON CARNE**

Ingredient	Recipe Quantity	AP Quantity	Price	Total Amount
Onion, EP*	2½ lb	_____	_____	_____
Green pepper, EP*	1¼ lb	_____	_____	_____
Vegetable oil	4 oz	_____	_____	_____
Ground beef	5 lb	_____	_____	_____
Tomatoes	#10 can	_____	_____	_____
Tomato paste	10 oz	_____	_____	_____
Beef stock	2½ pt	_____	_____	_____
Chili powder	3 oz	_____	_____	_____
			Total cost	_____
			Number of portions	24
			Cost per portion	_____

Note: Remember that you need AP weights of all ingredients (see pages 115 and 119 in the text). Let's assume that you kept a record of the quantities needed when you made this recipe:

To get 2½ lb EP onions, you needed 2 lb 12 oz AP.
To get 1¼ lb EP green pepper, you needed 1½ lb AP.

Portion Cost—Metric

Cost out the following recipe. For prices of the ingredients, use figures supplied by your instructor or the *Sample Prices* in the Appendix of this *Study Guide*.

ITEM: **CHILE CON CARNE**

Ingredient	Recipe Quantity	AP Quantity	Price	Total Amount
Onion, EP*	1.25 kg	_____	_____	_____
Green pepper, EP*	600 g	_____	_____	_____
Vegetable oil	125 mL	_____	_____	_____
Ground beef	2.5 kg	_____	_____	_____
Tomatoes	#10 can	_____	_____	_____
Tomato paste	300 g	_____	_____	_____
Beef stock	1.25 L	_____	_____	_____
Chili powder	100 g	_____	_____	_____

Total cost _____

Number of portions 24

Cost per portion _____

Note: Remember that you need AP weights of all ingredients (see pages 115 and 119 in the text). Let's assume that you kept a record of the quantities needed when you made this recipe:

To get 1.25 kg EP onions, you needed 1.5 kg AP.
To get 600 g EP green pepper, you needed 700 g AP.

Chapter 12

Understanding Poultry and Game Birds

The subject of poultry is divided into two chapters, just as the subject of meats is. Unlike the first meat chapter, however, this first poultry chapter is quite short. One of the reasons for this is that there is not such a great variety of different cuts of poultry to learn as there is for meats. Furthermore, much of this chapter is taken up with trussing and cutting techniques, which need hands-on practice rather than written study questions.

After studying Chapter 12, you should be able to:

1. Explain the differences between light meat and dark meat, and describe how these differences affect cooking.
2. Describe four techniques that help keep chicken or turkey breast moist while roasting.
3. Define the following terms used to classify poultry: *kind*, *class*, and *style*.
4. Identify popular types of farm-raised game birds and the cooking methods appropriate to their preparation.
5. Store poultry items.
6. Determine doneness in cooked poultry, both large roasted birds and smaller birds.
7. Truss poultry for cooking.
8. Cut chicken into parts.

A. Terms

Fill in each blank with the term that is defined or described.

_____ 1. A government procedure that checks the wholesomeness of poultry, to make sure that it is fit to eat.

_____ 2. A government procedure that checks the quality of poultry.

_____   **3.** The market term indicating the amount of cleaning and processing a poultry item has had.

_____   **4.** The market term indicating the species (such as chicken, turkey, or duck) of a poultry item.

_____   **5.** The market term that indicates the relative age and sometimes the sex of a poultry item.

_____   **6.** A castrated male chicken.

_____   **7.** A mature female chicken.

_____   **8.** A mature male chicken.

_____   **9.** A young pigeon.

_____   **10.** A type of domestic poultry related to the pheasant.

_____   **11.** The process of tying the legs and wings of a poultry item against the body to make a compact shape for cooking.

_____   **12.** A common name for the nugget of tender meat in the hollow of the hip bone.

_____   **13.** A special breed of young chicken, often marketed at about 1 lb in weight.

_____   **14.** The boneless breast of a moulard duck.

_____   **15.** A semi-boneless poultry breast with the wing bone left in.

B. Short-Answer Questions

1. A mature chicken of about 10 months of age is almost always cooked by what kind of cooking method? _____

2. Which of the major parts of a chicken has the most connective tissue? _____

3. The highest government grade of chicken is _____ .

4. What is the best way to thaw a frozen capon that is vacuum packed in plastic? _____

_____

5. What is the weight range for young turkey? _____

6. What class of duck is best for roasting, and what does one of these ducks weigh? _____

7. At what temperature should frozen turkey be stored? _____

8. A large roasted bird is done when a meat thermometer inserted into _____

registers the temperature of _____ .

9. Which disease-causing bacteria is most often associated with poultry? _____ What precaution

should be taken to avoid spreading this disease? _____

_____

10. What is the best way to hold fresh chickens in storage?

_____

11. A chicken or other poultry item that is raised without various chemical growth enhancers or without certain

antibiotics may be labeled _____ .

12. A chicken that is allowed to move around freely and eat outdoors in a more "natural" environment is called a

_____ chicken.

13. Two examples of ratites that appear on some menus are _____ and _____ .

14. The game bird discussed in Chapter 12 that is closest to chicken in size and flavor is _____ .

15. If you were serving breast of wild duck on your menu, you would recommend to customers that it should be

cooked to the _____ stage of doneness because _____

_____ .

16. The protein in the muscles of poultry that makes "dark meat" dark is called _____ .

The purpose of this protein is to _____ ,

therefore it is found in _____ (more active or less active) muscles.

Chapter 13

Cooking Poultry and Game Birds

In this chapter, our examination shifts from product information to cooking techniques. The basic cooking methods, first discussed in Chapter 4, are applied to a range of poultry items.

After studying Chapter 13, you should be able to:

1. Cook poultry by roasting and baking.
2. Cook poultry by broiling and grilling.
3. Cook poultry by sautéing, pan-frying, and deep-frying.
4. Cook poultry by simmering and poaching.
5. Cook poultry by braising.
6. Identify the safety, quality, and practicality concerns associated with preparing dressings and stuffings.
7. List basic ingredients for dressings and stuffings.
8. Prepare dressings and stuffings.

A. Terms

Fill in each blank with the term that is defined or described.

_____ 1. A chicken stew that is served with a pastry cover.

_____ 2. A white chicken stew cooked by the braising method, but without browning the chicken, and served in a white sauce.

_____ 3. A chicken stew prepared by the simmering method and served in a white sauce.

_____ 4. A chicken stew as described in number 3, garnished with asparagus tips.

_____ 5. A mature female chicken, which must be cooked by a moist-heat method to be made tender.

_____   6. Chicken braised in red wine, garnished with small onions, mushrooms, and bacon.

_____   7. Poultry that has been marinated, cooked in its own fat, then packed and stored in its own fat.

_____   8. Grilled or sautéed poultry, meat, or seafood glazed with a soy sauce mixture.

_____   9. Chicken served with a brown sauce flavored with white wine, shallots, mushrooms, and tomatoes.

_____   10. The side of a piece of food that is to be face up on a plate when served.

_____   11. A boneless chicken breast that has been pounded flat and then grilled.

_____   12. A dish made of boneless chicken breast meat that has been chopped, mixed with heavy cream, molded into cutlet shapes, and pan-fried.

_____   13. Classic French name for braised chicken with apples and cider.

_____   14. A term for a stuffed boneless chicken leg.

_____   15. Classic Spanish dish of chicken braised with rice.

_____   16. Any of a variety of complex Mexican sauces that are cooked with chiles and other spices and that are usually thickened with corn or ground seeds or nuts.

_____   17. To cook, covered, in an oven, basting regularly with butter, usually with a matignon for flavoring. Sometimes called *butter-roasting*.

B. Short-Answer Questions

1. What size chicken is best for deep-frying? _____

_____

2. When you are sautéing a boneless breast of chicken, which side of the chicken breast should be browned first, for best appearance? _____

3. At what oven temperature should a 5-lb (2.3-kg) chicken be roasted? _____

4. A basic bread dressing or stuffing is made of _____ , _____ ,

_____ , and _____ , plus herbs, seasonings, and sometimes eggs.

5. If a chicken is stuffed before roasting, it is necessary to _____ the roasting time.

6. Baked, refrigerated poultry dressing that is to be heated for service must be reheated to an internal temperature

of _____ . The reason for this is _____

_____ .

7. _____ is a cooking method similar to simmering but requiring less liquid and a lower temperature.

8. To "flash-roast" a cornish game hen means to _____ .

9. A good temperature range for roasting large birds such as turkeys is _____ .

10. In a classic chicken fricassée, the sauce is enriched by adding a _____ , and it is seasoned with salt, white pepper, a little nutmeg, and lemon juice.

11. If grilled chicken becomes well browned on the outside before it is completely cooked on the inside, it may be finished by removing it from the grill and _____
_____ .

12. The deep-fryer should be set at a temperature of _____ for deep-frying chicken.

13. Very small poultry items are generally roasted at a _____ temperature.

14. To "smoke-roast" a chicken breast means to _____
_____ .

15. Sautéed dishes made from game birds are most often made with the _____ section of the bird only.

They are usually cooked to the _____ stage of doneness.

C. Recipe Conversion

The following ingredients and quantities are for a Chicken à la King recipe that yields 25 portions at 8 oz each. Convert the recipe to the yields indicated.

	25 portions, 8 oz each	10 portions, 8 oz each	15 portions, 10 oz each
Butter, clarified	10 oz		
Onion	3 oz		
Green pepper	10 oz		
Flour	8 oz		
Chicken stock	2½ qt		
Milk	2½ cups		
Mushrooms	1 lb		
Butter	4 oz		
Light cream	2½ cups		
Pimientos, drained	4 oz		
Cooked chicken meat	5 lb		
Sherry wine	4 oz		
Salt	to taste		
Pepper	to taste		

Recipe Conversion—Metric

The following ingredients and quantities are for a Chicken à la King recipe that yields 25 portions at 250 g each. Convert the recipe to the yields indicated.

	25 portions, 250 g each	10 portions, 250 g each	15 portions, 300 g each
Butter, clarified	300 g		
Onion	100 g		
Green pepper	300 g		
Flour	250 g		
Chicken stock	2.5 L		
Milk	650 mL		
Mushrooms	500 g		
Butter	125 g		
Light cream	600 mL		
Pimientos, drained	124 g		
Cooked chicken meat	2.5 kg		
Sherry wine	125 mL		
Salt	to taste		
Pepper	to taste		

D. Portion Cost

In order to cost out the following recipe, we need to know the cost of cooked chicken meat. But let's assume we purchased and cooked fresh fowls in order to make the recipe. In order to cost the recipe, we first must do a cooked yield test, as discussed in Chapter 5 of the textbook, pages 118–119.

In the following shortened version of the cooked yield test form, use the figures given to calculate the cost per pound of the cooked chicken. Then use this figure to cost the recipe.

ITEM: **SIMMERED FRESH FOWL**

Net raw weight: 5 lb 4 oz   Cost per lb (raw): $ .89

Total net cost: $4.67

Weight as served (cooked meat): 1 lb 12 oz

Cooked cost per pound: _____

Cost out the following recipe. For prices of the ingredients, use figures supplied by your instructor or the *Sample Prices* in the Appendix of this *Study Guide*.

ITEM: **CHICKEN TETRAZZINI**

Ingredient	Recipe Quantity	AP Quantity	Price	Total Amount
Cooked chicken	5 lb	_____	_____	_____
Chicken stock	2½ qt	_____	_____	_____
Flour	4 oz	_____	_____	_____
Butter	10 oz	_____	_____	_____
Mushrooms	2 lb	_____	_____	_____
Egg yolks*	3	_____	_____	_____
Heavy cream	2½ cups	_____	_____	_____
Sherry	2 oz	_____	_____	_____
Spaghetti	2½ lb	_____	_____	_____
Parmesan cheese	8 oz	_____	_____	_____

Total cost _____

Number of portions   40

Cost per portion _____

Note: For the sake of this exercise, use the cost of whole eggs as the cost of the yolks. If you then use the egg whites in another recipe, you would enter a cost of zero for the whites when costing that recipe. This is because you are accounting for the cost of the whole eggs in the chicken recipe.

Portion Cost—Metric

In order to cost out the following recipe, we need to know the cost of cooked chicken meat. But let's assume we purchased and cooked fresh fowls in order to make the recipe. In order to cost the recipe, we first must do a cooked yield test, as discussed in Chapter 5 of the textbook, pages 118–119.

In the following shortened version of the cooked yield test form, use the figures given to calculate the cost per pound of the cooked chicken. Then use this figure to cost the recipe.

ITEM: **SIMMERED FRESH FOWL**

Net raw weight: 2.4 kg   Cost per kg (raw): $1.95

                                           Total net cost: $4.68

Weight as served (cooked meat): 800 g

Cooked cost per kilogram: _____

Cost out the following recipe. For prices of the ingredients, use figures supplied by your instructor or the *Sample Prices* in the Appendix of this *Study Guide*.

ITEM: **CHICKEN TETRAZZINI**

Ingredient	Recipe Quantity	AP Quantity	Price	Total Amount
Cooked chicken	2.5 kg	_____	_____	_____
Chicken stock	2.5 L	_____	_____	_____
Flour	125 g	_____	_____	_____
Butter	300 g	_____	_____	_____
Mushrooms	1 kg	_____	_____	_____
Egg yolks*	3	_____	_____	_____
Heavy cream	600 mL	_____	_____	_____
Sherry	50 mL	_____	_____	_____
Spaghetti	1.25 kg	_____	_____	_____
Parmesan cheese	250 g	_____	_____	_____

Total cost   _____

Number of portions   40

Cost per portion   _____

Note: For the sake of this exercise, use the cost of whole eggs as the cost of the yolks. If you then use the egg whites in another recipe, you would enter a cost of zero for the whites when costing that recipe. This is because you are accounting for the cost of the whole eggs in the chicken recipe.

Chapter 14

Understanding Fish and Shellfish

The composition and structure of fish and seafood products is quite different from that of meat and poultry. Furthermore, fish products are much more perishable than meat is. Consequently, this subject requires special study, so that when you apply the basic cooking techniques to seafood products, you will be able to adjust them to fit these unique products.

After studying Chapter 14, you should be able to:

1. Explain how the cooking qualities of fish are affected by the lack of connective tissue.
2. Determine doneness in cooked fish.
3. Demonstrate the appropriate cooking methods for fat and lean fish.
4. List the seven basic market forms of fish.
5. Dress and fillet round fish and flat fish.
6. List and describe common varieties of saltwater and freshwater fin fish used in North American food service.
7. Identify the characteristics of fresh fish, and contrast them with characteristics of not-so-fresh fish.
8. Store fish and fish products.
9. Identify the popular varieties of shellfish and discuss their characteristics.
10. Outline the special safe handling and cooking procedures for shellfish.
11. Open clams and oysters, split lobster, and peel and devein shrimp.

A. Terms

Fill in each blank with the term that is defined or described.

Mollusks   **1.** The family of sea animals that includes soft animals that live inside a pair of hinged shells.

Crustaceans   **2.** The family of sea animals that have segmented shells and jointed legs.

littlenecks _____ **3.** The smallest size of Eastern hard-shell clams.

chowders _____ **4.** The largest size of Eastern hard-shell clams.

adductor muscle **5.** In bivalves (animals with a pair of hinged shells), the muscle that closes the shells.

tomalley _____ **6.** The pale green liver of a lobster.

king crab _____ **7.** The largest of the crabs.

coral _____ **8.** The roe or eggs of a lobster.

sleepers _____ **9.** The inactive, dying lobster.

Individually _____ **10.** The words that the abbreviation IQF stands for.

quick _____

frozen _____

Green shrimp _____ **11.** Market term for raw shrimp in the shell.

Soft-shell _____ **12.** A blue crab that was harvested just after it molted or shed its shell.

peeled _____ **13.** The words that the abbreviation PDC, as applied to shrimp, stands for.

deveined (remove vein)

Cooked _____

_____ **14.** Coated with a thin layer of ice when frozen, in order to prevent drying.

Crayfish _____ **15.** A fresh-water shellfish that looks like a small lobster.

langoustines/langostinos **16.** A small relative of the rock lobster, sometimes sold as rock shrimp.

Calamari _____ **17.** The Italian name for squid, often used on menus.

Cephalopods _____ **18.** The name for the family of mollusks that includes squid, cuttlefish, and octopus.

Surimi _____ **19.** The general name for a processed seafood product that is made by grinding lean, white fish and shaping it to resemble crab legs and other shellfish.

anadramous _____ **20.** Designating fish that live in salt water but that swim into fresh water to lay eggs.

Catadramous _____ **21.** Designating fish that live in fresh water but that swim into salt water to lay eggs.

B. Fin Fish: Market Forms

In the blanks, write the name of the market form that corresponds to the description and illustration.

1. _____Drawn_____ Viscera removed

2. _____Fillets_____ Boneless side of fish

3. _____Whole/round_____ Completely intact, as caught

4. _____Steaks_____ Cross-section slices

5. _____Dressed_____ Viscera, scales, head, tail, and fins removed

6. _Butterflied Fillet_ Both sides of fish joined, bones removed

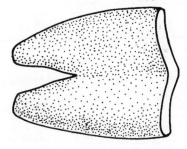

C. Fat Fish and Lean Fish

In the blank before the name of each fish, write the word "lean" if the fish is low in fat; write the word "fat" if it is high in fat.

1. _lean_____ Haddock
2. _Fat_____ Salmon
3. _lean_____ Ocean perch
4. _lean_____ Red snapper
5. _Fat_____ Tuna
6. _fat_____ Swordfish
7. _Fat_____ Pompano
8. _lean_____ Pike
9. _fat_____ Shad
10. _lean_____ Black sea bass
11. _Fat_____ Chilean sea bass
12. _lean_____ Whiting
13. _fat_____ Whitefish
14. _lean_____ Flounder
15. _lean_____ Sole
16. _lean_____ Cod
17. _fat_____ Escolar
18. _fat_____ Trout
19. _lean_____ Halibut
20. _fat_____ Bluefish
21. _fat_____ Mackerel
22. _lean_____ Tilefish
23. _lean_____ Monkfish
24. _fat_____ Eel
25. _lean_____ Skate
26. _lean_____ John Dory
27. _lean_____ Mahi-mahi
28. _lean_____ Red mullet
29. _lean_____ Tilapia

D. Review: Freshness and Storage

1. List five signs of freshness in whole fin fish.

   (a) _Good Apperence/clear slime/moist fins_

   (b) _Odor/fresh + mild/not strong fishy_

   (c) _eyes/clear shiny + buldging_

   (d) _Gills/red or pink_

   (e) _texture of flesh/firm + elastic_

2. What is the most important sign of freshness in fish fillets?

   Odor is fresh

3. What is the most important sign of freshness in lobsters?

   It is alive

4. What is the most important sign of freshness in clams, oysters, and mussels? ___

   alive + smell fresh

5. What is the best way to store whole fin fish?

   on crushed ice

6. At what temperature should frozen fish be stored?

   0° or colder

7. What is the best way to thaw frozen fish? _Refridgerator_

8. What is the best way to store fresh clams and oysters in the shell? _Keep in cold_

   wet place in the cartons or sacks in which thay arrived

9. What are two ways of storing live lobsters?

(a) _packed in moist seaweed or heavy paper in cool place_

(b) _In saltwater/tank_

10. What is the best way to store thawed raw shrimp in the shell?

on crushed ice like whole fish

E. True/False

T **(F)**   1. Haddock is an example of flatfish. _Saltwater/round_

(T) F   2. In general, fat fish are better suited for broiling than lean fish are.

T **(F)**   3. In fish cookery, moist-heat methods are used primarily to tenderize tough fish. _Preserve moistness_

T F   4. Some canned fish products are inspected for wholesomeness by the federal government.

T **(F)**   5. Shrimp that are designated "21/25" weigh about 1¼ oz each. _28_

T **(F)**   6. A fish that is very fresh has clear, white gills. _red or pink_

(T) F   7. The largest varieties of scallops are called sea scallops.

T **(F)**   8. Frozen fish fillets must be completely thawed before they can be breaded. _particially_

T **(F)**   9. Scallops are available only in the fall, winter, and spring. _all year_

T **(F)**   10. If baked clams are tough, it is because they weren't cooked long enough. _Cooked too long_

Chapter 15

Cooking Fish and Shellfish

This chapter applies the basic cooking techniques to seafood products. Keeping in mind that the structure of fish is quite different from that of meat and poultry, pay special attention to the ways in which cooking fish differs from cooking meats.

After studying Chapter 15, you should be able to:

1. Cook fish and shellfish by baking.
2. Cook fish and shellfish by broiling.
3. Cook fish and shellfish by sautéing and pan-frying.
4. Cook fish and shellfish by deep-frying.
5. Cook fish and shellfish by poaching in court bouillon.
6. Cook fish and shellfish by poaching in fumet and wine.
7. Cook fish and shellfish by mixed cooking techniques.
8. Prepare dishes made of raw seafood.

A. Terms

Fill in each blank with the term that is defined or described.

Court bouillon   1. Water containing seasonings, herbs, and usually an acid, used for cooking fish.

truite au bleu   2. Trout that was alive until cooking time and that turns blue when cooked in water containing an acid such as lemon juice or vinegar.

Fish tartare   3. A dish consisting of chopped raw fish mixed with seasoning.

à la meunière   4. Fish dredged in flour, sautéed in butter, and served with a topping of lemon juice, parsley, and browned butter.

Poached Fish Florentine   5. A dish consisting of poached fish on a bed of spinach, topped with Mornay sauce.

_____ **6.** A term referring to fish topped with a rich sauce and browned under a broiler or salamander.

Moules Marinière **7.** Mussels steamed with white wine, shallots, and parsley.

_____ **8.** A dish consisting of fish or seafood served in a cream sauce flavored with sherry or other fortified wine.

etuver **9.** A French term meaning "to cook a product in its own juices; to sweat."

en papillote **10.** Wrapped in paper for cooking so that the food is steamed in its own moisture.

paupiettes **11.** Thin, flat items such as fish fillets rolled up into tight rolls, then cooked and served in this fashion.

Sole vin Blanc **12.** French menu name for poached sole in white wine sauce.

_____ **13.** Dish similar to the one described in number 11, but with the addition of mushrooms.

_____ **14.** A dish consisting of trout prepared as described in number 3 but garnished with browned sliced almonds.

Lobster à l'Americaine **15.** A dish consisting of cut-up lobster sautéed and then cooked and served in a sauce made with tomato, shallot, garlic, white wine, brandy, fish stock, and herbs.

à la nage **16.** A style of preparation in which a poached fish or seafood item is served "swimming" in a broth made of its poaching liquid.

Tuna Carpaccio **17.** A dish consisting of thin slices of raw fish pounded paper-thin, served with a piquant cold sauce.

Cuisson **18.** French term for a cooking liquid.

Tempura **19.** A Japanese deep-fried dish characterized by a very light batter.

B. Review of Shallow Poaching Fish in Wine

The following are the steps in the procedure for poaching fish in wine and fish stock, but they are out of order. Place them in the correct order by writing the number "1" in front of the first step, "2" in front of the second step, and so on.

2 Butter the bottom of the pan.

9 Reduce the poaching liquid to about one-fourth of its volume.

12 Strain the sauce.

3 Sprinkle chopped shallots into the pan.

5 Add enough fish fumet and white wine to almost cover the fish.

_____11_____ Monter au beurre. Season with salt, white pepper, and lemon juice.

_____1_____ Collect all equipment and food supplies.

_____13_____ Plate the fish and coat with the sauce.

_____6_____ Cover the fish and bring the liquid to a simmer.

_____4_____ Arrange the fish portions in the pan in a single layer. Season them lightly.

_____7_____ Poach the fish, covered, in the oven or on the range at moderate heat.

_____10_____ Add fish velouté and heavy cream. Bring to a simmer and season with salt, white pepper, and lemon juice.

_____8_____ Drain the poaching liquid into another pan. Keep the fish warm.

_____ Add a tempered liaison.

C. Short-Answer Questions

1. When you are sautéing a fillet of fish, which side of the fillet should be browned first? _____

   ___Presentation Side___.

2. The breading on deep-fried fish serves several purposes. List three purposes.

   (a) ___Protect it from frying fat___

   (b) ___provides crisp, flavorful, + attractive coating___

   (c) ___protect frying fat from fish.___

3. Besides mirepoix and various seasonings, herbs, and spices, the two main ingredients in a court bouillon

   for cooking fish are ___Wine___ and ___Vinegar___.

4. Plain fish steaks to be baked or broiled are usually coated with ___Oil or butter___ before cooking.

5. What is the normal oven temperature range for baking fish? ___350-400___

6. The main flavoring ingredient for scampi-style broiled shrimp is ___lemon juice___.

7. Whole fish to be served cold on a buffet are usually cooked by what method? _____

8. When you are rolling up sole fillets to prepare them for cooking, which side of the fillet should be on the

   inside of the roll? ___Skin Side___

9. The preferred fats for sautéing fish are oil and ___butter___.

10. Fish to be sautéed à la meunière is often soaked in ___milk___ before dredging it in

    ___flour___. This helps form a crust that browns nicely.

11. List five guidelines for food safety when preparing and serving dishes made of raw seafood.

(a) _Use only freshest fish_

(b) _buy from reliable purveyor_

(c) _Use only saltwater fish from clean waters_

(d) _Observe strictest sanitation procedure_

(e) _keep fish cold & handle as little as possible_

12. The main ingredient in sushi is _rice_ .

13. _Seviche_ is a dish made by marinating raw seafood in _acid mixture_ until it has the texture of cooked fish.

D. Recipe Conversion

The following ingredients and quantities are for a Baked Clam recipe that yields 10 portions at 3 clams each. Convert the recipe to the yields indicated.

	10 portions, 3 clams each	30 portions, 3 clams each	30 portions, 4 clams each
Cherrystone clams	30	90	
Olive oil	2 oz	6 oz	
Shallots	1½ oz	4.5 oz	
Garlic, chopped	1 tsp	1 Tbsp	
Lemon juice	5 tsp	5 Tbsp	
Bread crumbs, fresh	10 oz	30 oz or 1 lb 14 oz	
Chopped parsley	1 tbsp	3 Tbsp	
Oregano	¾ tsp		
White pepper	⅛ tsp		
Parmesan cheese	⅓ cup		
Lemon wedges	10	30	

Recipe Conversion—Metric

The following ingredients and quantities are for a Baked Clam recipe that yields 10 portions at 3 clams each. Convert the recipe to the yields indicated.

	10 portions, 3 clams each	30 portions, 3 clams each	30 portions, 4 clams each
Cherrystone clams	30		
Olive oil	60 mL		
Shallots	50 g		
Garlic, chopped	5 mL		
Lemon juice	25 mL		
Bread crumbs, fresh	300 g		
Chopped parsley	15 mL		
Oregano	3 mL		
White pepper	0.5 mL		
Parmesan cheese	75 mL		
Lemon wedges	10		

E. Portion Cost

Cost out the following recipe. For prices of the ingredients, use figures supplied by your instructor or the *Sample Prices* in the Appendix of this *Study Guide*.

ITEM: **POACHED SOLE FILLETS BONNE FEMME**

Ingredient	Recipe Quantity	AP Quantity	Price	Total Amount
Sole fillets	6¼ lb	_____	_____	_____
Butter	7 oz	_____	_____	_____
Flour	4 oz	_____	_____	_____
Fish stock	3 cups	_____	_____	_____
Shallots*	3 oz	_____	_____	_____
Mushrooms*	1½ lb	_____	_____	_____
Heavy cream	12 oz	_____	_____	_____

Total cost _____

Number of portions   25

Cost per portion _____

Note: Remember that you need AP weights of all ingredients (see pages 115 and 119 in the text). Let's assume that you kept a record of the quantities needed when you made this recipe:

To get 3 oz EP shallots, you needed 4 oz AP.

To get 1½ lb EP mushrooms, you needed 1 lb 10 oz AP.

Portion Cost—Metric

Cost out the following recipe. For prices of the ingredients, use figures supplied by your instructor or the *Sample Prices* in the Appendix of this *Study Guide*.

ITEM: **POACHED SOLE FILLETS BONNE FEMME**

Ingredient	Recipe Quantity	AP Quantity	Price	Total Amount
Sole fillets	3 kg	_____	_____	_____
Butter	200 g	_____	_____	_____
Flour	125 g	_____	_____	_____
Fish stock	750 mL	_____	_____	_____
Shallots*	100 g	_____	_____	_____
Mushrooms*	700 g	_____	_____	_____
Heavy cream	350 mL	_____	_____	_____
			Total cost	_____
			Number of portions	25
			Cost per portion	_____

Note: Remember that you need AP weights of all ingredients (see pages 115 and 119 in the text). Let's assume that you kept a record of the quantities needed when you made this recipe:

To get 100 g EP shallots, you needed 125 g AP.

To get 700 g EP mushrooms, you needed 750 g AP.

Chapter 16

Understanding Vegetables

The material on vegetables and starches is divided into four chapters. While each of these four chapters of exercises is relatively short, together they contain many important points to study and review.

After studying Chapter 16, you should be able to:

1. Describe the factors that influence texture, flavor, color, and nutritional changes when cooking vegetables.

2. Cook vegetables to their proper doneness.

3. Judge quality in cooked vegetables based on color, appearance, texture, flavor, seasonings, and appropriateness of combination with sauces or other vegetables.

4. Perform pre-preparation tasks for fresh vegetables.

5. Determine the quality of frozen, canned, and dried vegetables.

6. Prepare vegetables using the batch cooking method and the blanch-and-chill method.

7. Store both fresh and processed vegetables.

A. Terms

Fill in each blank with the term that is defined or described.

_____ 1. Compounds that give vegetables their color.

_____ 2. Firm to the bite, not soft or mushy; a term used to describe the texture of vegetables and some other foods that are cooked to this stage of doneness.

_____ 3. The compound that colors green vegetables green.

_____ 4. The weight of the solids, minus the juice, in a can of vegetables or fruits.

_____ 5. The size of the individual pieces in a can of vegetables (for example, the diameter of the peas in a can).

_____ 6. The compounds that color carrots and sweet potatoes orange.

_____ 7. The compounds that color tomatoes and red peppers red.

_____ 8. The compounds that color corn yellow.

_____ 9. The compounds that color beets and red cabbage red.

_____ 10. The compounds that color cauliflower and potatoes white.

_____ 11. The fuzzy center of an artichoke.

_____ 12. Dried, discolored spots on frozen foods due to improper storage or packaging.

_____ 13. A kitchen procedure that involves dividing a large quantity of a food item into several smaller containers and cooking each one separately as needed.

_____ 14. A kitchen procedure that involves partially cooking foods ahead of time, refrigerating them, then finishing portions of the foods as needed at service time.

_____ 15. A mature cremini mushroom with a cap that forms a broad, thick, flat disk that may be as large as 6 inches (15 cm) or more across.

_____ 16. A popular wild mushroom that is cone-shaped and hollow.

_____ 17. The fresh version of the dried Chinese black mushroom.

_____ 18. A golden-yellow wild mushroom shaped like an inside-out umbrella and with ridges instead of gills.

B. Short-Answer Questions

1. If green beans are cooked with lemon juice, their color will turn _____ .

2. When peas are harvested, their _____ content begins to change to starch.

3. Frozen vegetables should be stored at a temperature of _____ .

4. Baking soda added to cooking water makes the texture of vegetables _____ .

5. Cut surfaces of artichokes are rubbed with _____ so that they will not turn brown.

6. Rutabagas should be cooked uncovered so that _____

_____ .

7. The top of a can of vegetables should be _____ before it is opened.

8. A bulging can of green beans should be _____ .

9. Vitamins in vegetables can be lost or destroyed by

(a) _____ ,   (b) _____ ,

(c) _____ ,   (d) _____ ,

(e) _____ , and (f) _____ .

10. Vegetables should be cut into neat, uniform shapes for better appearance and for _____ .

11. When fresh peas are added to cooking water, the temperature of the water should be _____ .

12. The bottom portions of asparagus stalks are _____ so that the asparagus will cook more evenly.

13. Frozen vegetables need less cooking time than fresh vegetables because _____ .

14. Two or more batches of cooked vegetables should not be mixed together because _____

_____ .

15. Five examples of hot peppers or chiles are _____ , _____ , _____ , _____ ,

and _____ .

16. Before dried mushrooms are used in a recipe, they should be _____

_____ .

17. The most important reason never to use a wild mushroom that hasn't been definitely identified by an expert is

_____ .

C. Math Exercise: Trimming Loss

The exercises below are of two kinds, calculating yield and calculating amount needed. To do the calculations, you need to know the percentage yield for each vegetable, as listed in Chapter 16 of the text. For your convenience, the necessary percentages are repeated here.

These calculations are explained in Chapter 5 of the text, in the section titled "Trimming Loss: Calculating Yields and Amounts Needed." Review this section if necessary.

Artichokes, Jerusalem	80%
Asparagus	55%
Beans, green	88%
Broccoli	70%
Cabbage	80%
Celery	75%

Eggplant	75% (peeled)
Kohlrabi	55%
Leeks	50%
Mushrooms	90%
Okra	82%
Onions, dry	90%
Peas	40%
Potatoes	80%
Turnips	75%
Zucchini	90%

Calculating Amount Needed

Assume you need the following quantities, EP, of the indicated fresh vegetables. Calculate the AP weight you will need to get the required yield. (Questions 1–10 use U.S. measures; questions 11–20 use metric measures. Answer whichever questions are assigned by your instructor.)

	EP Weight Desired	AP Weight Needed
1. Kohlrabi	1 lb	_____
2. Potatoes	12 oz	_____
3. Jerusalem artichokes	1 lb	_____
4. Eggplant, peeled	2½ lb	_____
5. Leeks	6 oz	_____
6. Okra	8 oz	_____
7. Onions, dry	1½ lb	_____
8. Mushrooms	1 lb	_____
9. Celery	3 lb	_____
10. Zucchini	2 lb	_____

	EP Weight Desired	AP Weight Needed
11. Kohlrabi	500 g	_____
12. Potatoes	400 g	_____
13. Jerusalem artichokes	450 g	_____
14. Eggplant, peeled	1.25 kg	_____
15. Leeks	200 g	_____
16. Okra	250 g	_____
17. Onions, dry	700 g	_____
18. Mushrooms	475 g	_____
19. Celery	1.5 kg	_____
20. Zucchini	900 g	_____

Calculating Yield

Assume you have the following quantities, AP, of the indicated fresh vegetables. Calculate the EP weight you will have left after trimming. (Questions 21–30 use U.S. measures; questions 31–40 use metric measures. Answer whichever questions are assigned by your instructor.)

	AP Weight	EP Weight
21. Asparagus	12 oz	_____
22. Red cabbage	6 lb	_____
23. Mushrooms	2½ lb	_____
24. Green beans	1½ lb	_____
25. Peas	4½ lb	_____
26. Turnips	2 lb	_____
27. Broccoli	2½ lb	_____
28. Leeks	6 lb	_____
29. Okra	1 lb	_____
30. Zucchini	5 lb	_____
31. Asparagus	375 g	_____
32. Red cabbage	3 kg	_____
33. Mushrooms	1.25 kg	_____

34. Green beans   700 g   _____

35. Peas   2.2 kg   _____

36. Turnips   450 g   _____

37. Broccoli   1.2 kg   _____

38. Leeks   2.75 kg   _____

39. Okra   500 g   _____

40. Zucchini   2.75 kg   _____

Chapter 17

Cooking Vegetables

This chapter continues your review of vegetables, concentrating on cooking techniques. After studying Chapter 17, you should be able to:

1. Identify vegetables that are well suited to the different vegetable cooking methods.
2. Cook vegetables by boiling and steaming.
3. Cook vegetables by sautéing and pan-frying.
4. Cook vegetables by braising.
5. Cook vegetables by baking.
6. Cook vegetables by broiling and grilling.
7. Cook vegetables by deep-frying.

A. Terms

Fill in each blank with the term that is defined or described.

_____ 1. A style of vegetable preparation in which the vegetables are topped with browned sliced almonds.

_____ 2. A style of vegetable preparation in which the vegetable preparation is covered with a topping, such as a sauce, cheese, and/or bread crumbs, and browned under a boiler or salamander.

_____ 3. A dish consisting of braised sauerkraut served with a variety of sausages and other pork products.

_____ 4. A general term referring to foods coated with or mixed with a batter and deep-fried.

_____ 5. To give a vegetable a shiny coating by cooking it with sugar and butter or with a syrup.

_____   6. Thick vegetable purées or mixtures of small pieces of vegetable and a heavy béchamel or other binder, formed into shapes, breaded, and fried.

_____   7. A style of vegetable preparation in which the vegetable is topped with chopped hard-cooked egg, chopped parsley, and bread crumbs browned in butter.

_____   8. A vegetable stew made of eggplant, tomatoes, onions, peppers, and zucchini.

_____   9. Artichoke bottoms filled with peas.

_____   10. A coarse paste or hash made of finely chopped mushrooms sautéed with shallots.

_____   11. Peas cooked with pearl onions and shredded lettuce in a lightly bound white stock.

_____   12. A method of cooking vegetables in a small amount of water in a covered pan so that they partly steam and partly boil.

B. True/False

T   F   1. One advantage of cooking vegetables in a pressure steamer is that the door can be opened at any time to check on the vegetables.

T   F   2. Simmering is better than boiling for vegetables that can be easily broken.

T   F   3. If green peas are not to be served soon after they are boiled, they should be cooled in cold water and refrigerated until needed.

T   F   4. Zucchini must be parboiled before being sautéed.

T   F   5. Sautéing is similar to pan-frying, except that sautéing always requires more fat.

T   F   6. To sauté vegetables, set the sauté pan over moderate heat, add the butter and vegetables, then wait until the pan gets hot before flipping the vegetables.

T   F   7. Braised vegetables are browned in fat, then cooked slowly in a small amount of liquid.

T   F   8. The difference between braised meat and braised vegetables is that mirepoix is never used with vegetables.

T   F   9. Vinegar is added to braised red cabbage to flavor it and to enhance its red color.

T   F   10. Quick-cooking vegetables are best for broiling.

T   F   11. All vegetables that are coated in batter and deep-fried must first be blanched or parboiled.

T   F   12. Deep-fried vegetables are best if cooked to order.

T   F   13. Perforated pans should never be used for steaming vegetables, because too many juices will be lost.

T   F   14. Creamed spinach is made by cooking fresh spinach in a cream sauce.

C. Recipe Conversion

The following ingredients and quantities are for a Braised Red Cabbage recipe that yields 25 portions at 5 oz each. Convert the recipe to the yields indicated.

	25 portions, 5 oz each	10 portions, 5 oz each	15 portions, 4 oz each
Red cabbage, AP	6 lb		
Bacon	12 oz		
Onions	1 lb		
Sugar	1 oz		
White stock	1½ pt		
Apples, cored and diced	1 lb		
Cloves	4		
Whole allspice	6		
Stick cinnamon	1 piece		
Red wine vinegar	4 oz		
Red wine	1 cup		
Salt	to taste		
Pepper	to taste		

Recipe Conversion—Metric

The following ingredients and quantities are for a Braised Red Cabbage recipe that yields 25 portions at 125 g each. Convert the recipe to the yields indicated.

	25 portions, 125 g each	10 portions, 125 g each	15 portions, 100 g each
Red cabbage, AP	2.5 kg	_____	_____
Bacon	350 g	_____	_____
Onions	400 g	_____	_____
Sugar	25 g	_____	_____
White stock	700 mL	_____	_____
Apples, cored and diced	400 g	_____	_____
Cloves	4	_____	_____
Whole allspice	6	_____	_____
Stick cinnamon	1 piece	_____	_____
Red wine vinegar	100 mL	_____	_____
Red wine	250 mL	_____	_____
Salt	to taste	_____	_____
Pepper	to taste	_____	_____

D. Portion Cost

Cost out the following recipes. For prices of the ingredients, use figures supplied by your instructor or the *Sample Prices* in the Appendix of this *Study Guide*.

ITEM: **ARTICHOKES CLAMART**

Ingredient	Recipe Quantity	AP Quantity	Price	Total Amount
Artichokes	10	_____	_____	_____
Lemons	2	_____	_____	_____
Flour	1 oz	_____	_____	_____
Cold water	3 pt	_____	_____	_____
Salt	½ oz	_____	_____	_____
Peas, frozen	10 oz	_____	_____	_____
Butter	3 oz	_____	_____	_____
			Total cost	_____
			Number of portions	10
			Cost per portion	_____

ITEM: **GLAZED CARROTS**

Ingredient	Recipe Quantity	AP Quantity	Price	Total Amount
Carrots, AP	6½ lb	_____	_____	_____
Butter	3 oz	_____	_____	_____
Sugar	2 oz	_____	_____	_____
			Total cost	_____
			Number of portions	25
			Cost per portion	_____

ITEM: **PUREED BUTTERNUT SQUASH**

Ingredient	Recipe Quantity	AP Quantity	Price	Total Amount
Butternut squash	10 lb	_____	_____	_____
Butter	8 oz	_____	_____	_____
Brown sugar	4 oz	_____	_____	_____
Salt	½ oz	_____	_____	_____
			Total cost	_____
			Number of portions	25
			Cost per portion	_____

Portion Cost—Metric

Cost out the following recipes. For prices of the ingredients, use figures supplied by your instructor or the *Sample Prices* in the Appendix of this *Study Guide*.

ITEM: **ARTICHOKES CLAMART**

Ingredient	Recipe Quantity	AP Quantity	Price	Total Amount
Artichokes	10	_____	_____	_____
Lemons	2	_____	_____	_____
Flour	30 g	_____	_____	_____
Cold water	1.5 l	_____	_____	_____
Salt	15 g	_____	_____	_____
Peas, frozen	300 g	_____	_____	_____
Butter	90 g	_____	_____	_____
			Total cost	_____
			Number of portions	10
			Cost per portion	_____

ITEM: **GLAZED CARROTS**

Ingredient	Recipe Quantity	AP Quantity	Price	Total Amount
Carrots, AP	3 kg	_____	_____	_____
Butter	100 g	_____	_____	_____
Sugar	60 g	_____	_____	_____
			Total cost	_____
			Number of portions 25	
			Cost per portion	_____

ITEM: **PUREED BUTTERNUT SQUASH**

Ingredient	Recipe Quantity	AP Quantity	Price	Total Amount
Butternut squash	5 kg	_____	_____	_____
Butter	250 g	_____	_____	_____
Brown sugar	125 g	_____	_____	_____
Salt	15 g	_____	_____	_____
			Total cost	_____
			Number of portions 25	
			Cost per portion	_____

Chapter 18

Potatoes

The last of three chapters covering basic vegetable cookery, this unit concentrates on potatoes. The importance of potatoes in our diet suggests that a thorough review of this material is important.

After studying Chapter 18, you should be able to:

1. Classify potatoes into two types, describe the general properties of each type, and identify the most suitable cooking method for each type.
2. Identify characteristics of high-quality potatoes, and describe how to store them.
3. Cook potatoes by boiling and steaming.
4. Prepare potato purée.
5. Cook potatoes by baking, sautéing, pan-frying, and deep-frying.

A. Terms

Fill in each blank with the term that is defined or described.

_____ 1. A variety of potato, often from Idaho, having a high starch content and often used for baking.

_____ 2. General term for potatoes that are low in starch and high in sugar, with a firm, moist texture.

_____ 3. A poisonous substance present in the green parts found in some potatoes.

_____ 4. Another name for immature potatoes.

_____ 5. Long, narrow, finger-shaped potato.

_____ 6. Name given to many classical dishes featuring the potato, after the French pharmacist who promoted the use of the potato in the eighteenth century.

_____ 7. Potato purée mixed with egg yolk and butter, piped with a pastry bag and browned under a salamander.

B. Classic Potato Preparations

Column 1 below is a list of descriptions of various classic potato dishes. Column 2 is a list of the names of these dishes. Match the names to the descriptions by writing the letter of the correct name in the space before the description.

_____ 1. Potato purée combined with butter and egg yolks, often used for decorative work

_____ 2. Sliced potatoes baked with cream, milk, and cheese

_____ 3. Cooked potatoes chopped, formed into cakes, and pan-fried

_____ 4. Trimmed potatoes simmered in stock with onion and carrot

_____ 5. Mixture of duchesse potatoes and pâte à choux, deep-fried

_____ 6. Small tournéed potatoes browned in butter

_____ 7. Thin, matchstick-sized french fries

_____ 8. Plain boiled potatoes

_____ 9. Same as number 5 but flavored with parmesan cheese

_____ 10. Cut with ball cutter and browned in butter

_____ 11. Sliced potatoes arranged in overlapping rings in a pan and baked with butter

_____ 12. Sliced potatoes and onions moistened with stock and baked with roast lamb

_____ 13. Baked in cheese sauce until browned on top

_____ 14. Duchesse mixture shaped, breaded, and deep-fried

_____ 15. Sliced, boiled potatoes pan-fried with onions

_____ 16. Diced potatoes pan-fried with bacon, onion, green pepper, and pimiento

_____ 17. Steamed potatoes

_____ 18. Baked potatoes puréed with butter, made into cakes, and pan-fried

_____ 19. Boiled potatoes sliced and pan-fried

_____ 20. Potatoes sliced on a mandoline into waffle shapes, deep-fried until crisp

a. Rissolé or Cocotte
b. Dauphine Potatoes
c. Parisienne or Noisette
d. Duchesse Potatoes
e. au Gratin
f. Boulangère
g. Home Fries
h. O'Brien
i. Croquettes
j. Lyonnaise
k. Hashed Browns
l. Allumette
m. Dauphinoise
n. Anna
o. Bouillon
p. Gaufrette
q. Macaire
r. Pommes Vapeurs
s. Lorette
t. Pommes Natures

C. Short-Answer Questions

1. List six characteristics of a high-quality potato.

(a) _____

(b) _____

(c) _____

(d) _____

(e) _____

(f) _____

2. At what temperature should potatoes be stored? _____

3. The following are steps in the procedure for making potato purée for duchesse potatoes. Fill in the missing step.

(a) Wash, peel, and eye. Cut into uniform sizes.

(b) Simmer until tender.

(c) Drain in colander.

(d) _____

(e) Pass through a food mill to purée.

4. How are french fries blanched? _____

_____

_____

5. Why should starchy potatoes not be refrigerated? _____

_____

6. What is the easiest and most commonly used method for preventing potatoes from turning brown after they

have been peeled or cut? _____

_____

7. What kind of potatoes are most often used for making potato purée—starchy or waxy? _____

Why? _____

_____

8. What are the four principal colors of potatoes?

_____

_____

_____

_____

9. What is likely to happen to potato purée if it is mixed too much? _____

_____

D. Recipe Conversion

The following ingredients and quantities are for Hungarian Potatoes, yielding 25 portions, 4 oz each. Convert the recipe to the yields indicated.

	25 portions, 4 oz each	15 portions, 4 oz each	15 portions, 5 oz each
Butter	4 oz	_____	_____
Onion	8 oz	_____	_____
Paprika	2 tsp	_____	_____
Tomato concassée	1 lb	_____	_____
Potatoes, peeled	5 lb	_____	_____
Chicken stock	1 qt	_____	_____
Salt	to taste	_____	_____
Pepper	to taste	_____	_____
Chopped parsley	½ cup	_____	_____

The following ingredients and quantities are for a recipe for Potatoes au Gratin, yielding 25 portions at 6 oz each. Convert the recipe to the yields indicated.

	25 portions, 6 oz each	15 portions, 6 oz each	25 portions, 4 oz each
Potatoes, all-purpose	7½ lb	_____	_____
Cheese sauce	2 qt	_____	_____
Dry bread crumbs	⅔ cup	_____	_____
Paprika	2 tsp	_____	_____
Butter, melted	2 oz	_____	_____

Recipe Conversion—Metric

The following ingredients and quantities are for a recipe for Hungarian Potatoes, yielding 25 portions at 100 g each. Convert the recipe to the yields indicated.

	25 portions, 100 g each	15 portions, 100 g each	15 portions, 125 g each
Butter	100 g	_____	_____
Onion	200 g	_____	_____
Paprika	10 mL	_____	_____
Tomato concassée	400 g	_____	_____
Potatoes, peeled	2 kg	_____	_____
Chicken stock	800 mL	_____	_____
Salt	to taste	_____	_____
Pepper	to taste	_____	_____
Chopped parsley	100 mL	_____	_____

The following ingredients and quantities are for a recipe for Potatoes au Gratin, yielding 25 portions at 175 g each. Convert the recipe to the yields indicated.

	25 portions, 175 g each	15 portions, 175 g each	25 portions, 125 g each
Potatoes, all-purpose	3.5 kg	_____	_____
Cheese sauce	2 L	_____	_____
Dry bread crumbs	150 mL	_____	_____
Paprika	10 mL	_____	_____
Butter, melted	60 g	_____	_____

E. Portion Cost

Cost out the following recipes. For prices of the ingredients, use figures supplied by your instructor or the *Sample Prices* in the Appendix of this *Study Guide*.

ITEM: **BOULANGERE POTATOES**

Ingredient	Recipe Quantity	AP Quantity	Price	Total Amount
Onions, AP	2½ lb	_____	_____	_____
Butter	5 oz	_____	_____	_____
Potatoes, all-purpose, AP	7½ lb	_____	_____	_____
Chicken stock	1 qt	_____	_____	_____
			Total cost	_____
			Number of portions	25
			Cost per portion	_____

ITEM: **POTATO PANCAKES**

Ingredient	Recipe Quantity	AP Quantity	Price	Total Amount
Potatoes, all-purpose	6 lb	_____	_____	_____
Onions	1 lb	_____	_____	_____
Lemons	2	_____	_____	_____
Eggs	6	_____	_____	_____
Flour, all-purpose	2 oz	_____	_____	_____
			Total cost	_____
			Number of portions	20
			Cost per portion	_____

Portion Cost—Metric

Cost out the following recipes. For prices of the ingredients, use figures supplied by your instructor or the *Sample Prices* in the Appendix of this *Study Guide*.

ITEM: **BOULANGERE POTATOES**

Ingredient	Recipe Quantity	AP Quantity	Price	Total Amount
Onions, AP	1.2 kg			
Butter	150 g			
Potatoes, all-purpose, AP	3.6 kg			
Chicken stock	1 L			

Total cost _____

Number of portions   25

Cost per portion _____

ITEM: **POTATO PANCAKES**

Ingredient	Recipe Quantity	AP Quantity	Price	Total Amount
Potatoes, all-purpose	2.7 kg			
Onions	450 g			
Lemons	2			
Eggs	6			
Flour, all-purpose	60 g			

Total cost _____

Number of portions   20

Cost per portion _____

Chapter 19

Legumes, Grains, Pasta, and Other Starches

This chapter continues the study of starch products that was begun with the discussion of potatoes in Chapter 18. The three main sections in this chapter are dried legumes, grains, and pasta or noodle products. In addition, various dumplings are introduced.

After studying Chapter 19, you should be able to:

1. Distinguish the major types of dried legumes.
2. Cook dried legumes.
3. Distinguish the major types of rice.
4. Distinguish the major types of other grains used in food service.
5. Prepare grains by simmering and by the pilaf and risotto methods.
6. Distinguish major kinds and shapes of commercial pasta and determine their quality.
7. Prepare fresh and commercial pasta products, and list the steps involved in the alternate steam-table method of its preparation.

A. Terms

Fill in each blank with the term that is defined or described.

_____ **1.** Rice that is first cooked in fat, then in liquid; braised rice.

_____ **2.** Firm, not soft or mushy; a term often used to describe the doneness of properly cooked pasta.

_____ **3.** A plant that bears seed pods that split along two opposite sides when ripe. Also, the seed from such a plant, used as food.

_____ **4.** A variety of short-grain rice from Italy.

_____   **5.** Seeds from various types of green beans.

_____   **6.** An extra-long-grain rice from India, with a distinctive nutty flavor.

_____   **7.** Mexican whole-grain hominy.

_____   **8.** A paste made of fresh basil and other ingredients, often used as a pasta sauce.

_____   **9.** The generic Indian term for dried legume.

_____   **10.** An Asian sweet-tasting short-grain rice that becomes quite sticky and chewy when cooked, usually by steaming.

_____   **11.** A granular pasta made from semolina wheat and cooked by soaking and then steaming. This product is often mistaken for a type of grain.

_____   **12.** A type of cracked wheat that has been partially cooked; often used in salads.

_____   **13.** An Italian rice dish made by adding stock a little at a time to rice in a pan and stirring constantly while it cooks.

_____   **14.** Rice with the bran left on.

_____   **15.** High-gluten flour used for the best-quality commercial macaroni products.

_____   **16.** Baked casserole made of wide, flat noodles layered with other products such as tomato sauce and cheese.

_____   **17.** Pillow-shaped stuffed egg noodles.

_____   **18.** Corn treated with lye and cracked into a coarse meal.

_____   **19.** An aromatic white rice from Thailand.

_____   **20.** A thin Japanese noodle made from buckwheat.

_____   **21.** A lens-shaped legume.

_____   **22.** The part of a whole grain that is the embryo of a new plant.

_____   **23.** The starchy mass that forms most of the kernel of a grain.

_____   **24.** The French location where the most prized green lentils are grown.

_____   **25.** Seafood product sometimes used to give a black color to pasta.

_____   **26.** Two names for a wheat-like grain that may be an ancient ancestor of modern
                                          wheat.

_____

_____   **27.** Thin noodles made with mung bean starch.

_____   **28.** Italian cornmeal.

B. Short-Answer Questions

1. Describe the basic cooking procedure for dried kidney beans. Use numbered steps.

_____

_____

_____

_____

_____

_____

_____

_____

_____

_____

2. What is the main difference between the procedure for split peas and the procedure for cooking dried kidney

   beans? _____

   _____

3. The four main parts of a whole grain are _____ , _____ ,

   _____ , and _____ . The part that forms the largest portion of the grain

   is the _____ .

4. Glutinous rice is usually cooked by what cooking method? _____ . Before it can be cooked

   by this method, it must first be _____ .

5. What legume has the most high-quality protein? _____

6. What is parboiled rice? _____

_____

7. Which kind of rice is most often used as a side dish—short grain, medium grain, or long grain? _____

8. If you are making pilaf with 1 qt (or 1 L) of raw rice, how much stock will you need? _____

9. To cook 1 lb of spaghetti, how much water do you need? _____

10. To get three 10-oz portions (or, if you use metric units, three 300-g portions) of cooked spaghetti, about how much dry, commercial spaghetti do you need? _____

11. What is the purpose of washing white rice before boiling it? _____

_____

12. Describe the procedure for preparing or cooking rice noodles for use in stir-fried dishes.

_____

_____

_____

_____

C. Pasta Shapes

In the space before the name of each pasta shape, write the letter of the illustration that corresponds.

_____ 1. Fusilli

_____ 2. Ditalini

_____ 3. Spaghettini

_____ 4. Lasagne

_____ 5. Penne

_____ 6. Orzo

_____ 7. Stelline

_____ 8. Ziti

_____ 9. Conchiglie

_____ 10. Elbow macaroni

_____ 11. Fettuccine

_____ 12. Manicotti

D. Recipe Conversion

The following ingredients and quantities are for a recipe for Pesto, yielding 12 portions at 2 oz each. Convert the recipe to the yields indicated.

	12 portions, 2 oz each	4 portions, 2 oz each	16 portions, 1½ oz each
Fresh basil leaves	2 qt	_____	_____
Olive oil	1½ cups	_____	_____
Pignoli	2 oz	_____	_____
Garlic cloves	6	_____	_____
Salt	1½ tsp	_____	_____
Parmesan cheese	5 oz	_____	_____
Romano cheese	1½ oz	_____	_____

The following ingredients and quantities are for a recipe for Pasta e Fagioli, yielding 12 portions, 8 fl oz each. Convert the recipe to the yields indicated.

	12 portions, 8 fl oz each	16 portions, 8 fl oz each	16 portions, 10 fl oz each
Dried cranberry beans	12 oz	_____	_____
Olive oil	4 fl oz	_____	_____
Pancetta	6 oz	_____	_____
Onion	6 oz	_____	_____
Carrot	6 oz	_____	_____
Celery	6 oz	_____	_____
Fresh sage leaves	4	_____	_____
Fresh rosemary	1 tbsp	_____	_____
Chopped parsley	3 tbsp	_____	_____
Water	2½ qt	_____	_____
Tomato paste	1 oz	_____	_____
Dried fettuccine	1 lb	_____	_____

Recipe Conversion—Metric

The following ingredients and quantities are for a recipe for Pesto, yielding 12 portions at 60 mL each. Convert the recipe to the yields indicated.

	12 portions, 60 mL each	4 portions, 60 mL each	16 portions, 45 mL each
Fresh basil leaves	2 L	_____	_____
Olive oil	375 mL	_____	_____
Pignoli	60 g	_____	_____
Garlic cloves	6	_____	_____
Salt	7 mL	_____	_____
Parmesan cheese	150 g	_____	_____
Romano cheese	45 g	_____	_____

The following ingredients and quantities are for a recipe for Pasta e Fagioli, yielding 12 portions at 240 mL each. Convert the recipe to the yields indicated.

	12 portions, 240 mL each	16 portions, 240 mL each	16 portions, 300 mL each
Dried cranberry beans	360 g	_____	_____
Olive oil	120 mL	_____	_____
Pancetta	180 g	_____	_____
Onion	180 g	_____	_____
Carrot	90 g	_____	_____
Celery	90 g	_____	_____
Fresh sage leaves	4	_____	_____
Fresh rosemary	15 mL	_____	_____
Chopped parsley	45 mL	_____	_____
Water	2.5 L	_____	_____
Tomato paste	30 g	_____	_____
Dried fettuccine	450 g	_____	_____

E. Portion Cost

Cost out the following recipes. For prices of the ingredients, use figures supplied by your instructor or the *Sample Prices* in the Appendix of this *Study Guide*.

ITEM: **FETTUCCINE ALFREDO**

Ingredient	Recipe Quantity	AP Quantity	Price	Total Amount
Fresh pasta				
Flour	1 lb	_____	_____	_____
Eggs	5	_____	_____	_____
Olive oil	½ oz	_____	_____	_____
Heavy cream	1 pt	_____	_____	_____
Butter	2 oz	_____	_____	_____
Parmesan cheese	6 oz	_____	_____	_____
			Total cost	_____
			Number of portions	10
			Cost per portion	_____

ITEM: **BULGUR PILAF**

Ingredient	Recipe Quantity	AP Quantity	Price	Total Amount
Butter	1 oz	_____	_____	_____
Onion, chopped fine	4 oz	_____	_____	_____
Bulgur, coarse	8 oz	_____	_____	_____
Chicken stock	1½ pt	_____	_____	_____
			Total cost	_____
			Number of portions	12
			Cost per portion	_____

Portion Cost—Metric

Cost out the following recipes. For prices of the ingredients, use figures supplied by your instructor or the *Sample Prices* in the Appendix of this *Study Guide*.

ITEM: **FETTUCCINE ALFREDO**

Ingredient	Recipe Quantity	AP Quantity	Price	Total Amount
Fresh pasta				
Flour	450 g	_____	_____	_____
Eggs	5	_____	_____	_____
Olive oil	15 mL	_____	_____	_____
Heavy cream	500 mL	_____	_____	_____
Butter	60 g	_____	_____	_____
Parmesan cheese	175 g	_____	_____	_____
			Total cost	_____
			Number of portions	10
			Cost per portion	_____

ITEM: **BULGUR PILAF**

Ingredient	Recipe Quantity	AP Quantity	Price	Total Amount
Butter	30 g	_____	_____	_____
Onion, chopped fine	125 g	_____	_____	_____
Bulgur, coarse	250 g	_____	_____	_____
Chicken stock	750 mL	_____	_____	_____
			Total cost	_____
			Number of portions	12
			Cost per portion	_____

Chapter 20

Cooking
for Vegetarian Diets

This chapter gives you the information you need in order to plan recipes and menus suitable for various styles of vegetarian diets.

After studying Chapter 20, you should be able to:

1. Describe the main types of vegetarian diets.
2. Describe complementary proteins and describe how to include them in the diet.
3. List three nutrients other than proteins that nonvegetarians get mostly from animal products, and describe how vegetarians can include these nutrients in their diets.
4. Name and describe five food types derived from soybeans.
5. Explain why refined sugar may not be permitted in a vegan diet.
6. List seven guidelines for building a vegetarian menu.

A. Terms

Fill in each blank with the term that is defined or described.

_____ 1. A compound or molecule that, when combined with similar compounds, makes up a protein molecule.

_____ 2. A paste made by fermenting soybeans and various grains.

_____ 3. A style of vegetarian diet that excludes all animal products.

_____ 4. A style of vegetarian diet that excludes all animal products except eggs and dairy products.

_____ 5. A style of vegetarian diet that excludes all animal products except eggs.

_____ 6. A style of vegetarian diet that excludes all animal products except dairy products.

_____ **7.** A style of vegetarian diet in which fish may be eaten.

_____ **8.** A protein food made from defatted soy flour, processed and dried to give it a spongelike texture, often flavored to taste like meat.

_____ **9.** A liquid product made by soaking dried soybeans, draining them, grinding them, combining them with water and bringing to a boil, and then straining.

_____ **10.** A product made by curdling the item described in number 9.

_____ **11.** A fermented soybean product, originating in Indonesia, with a dense, meaty texture.

_____ **12.** An amino acid that must be included in the diet in order for the body to get adequate protein.

_____ **13.** A protein or protein food that contains all the amino acids described in number 12.

_____ **14.** Protein foods that, when eaten together, supply all the amino acids described in number 12.

B. Short-Answer Questions

1. In addition to protein, what three nutrients, normally found in animal products, must be found in other sources in vegetarian diets and, thus, are of special concern? List as many nonanimal sources of these nutrients as you can.

Nutrient: _____

Sources: _____

_____

Nutrient: _____

Sources: _____

_____

Nutrient: _____

Sources: _____

_____

2. List three categories of foods that are valuable sources of protein in a vegan diet.

_____

_____

_____

3. In addition to the foods listed in question 2, list foods that a lacto-vegetarian can add to his or her diet to supply protein. _____

_____

4. Considering the subject of complementary proteins, explain the meaning of "limiting amino acid." _____

_____

_____

_____

5. Combine the following three kinds of foods into three groups that are good sources of complementary proteins:

Whole grains

Dried legumes

Milk products

_____

_____

_____

6. How many amino acids are considered "essential amino acids"? _____

7. Name and describe three types of tofu.

_____

_____

_____

8. Name three plant products that contain complete protein.

_____

_____

_____

9. Why are some sugar products avoided by many vegetarians? _____

_____

10. What sugar products can be included in vegetarian diets? _____

_____

C. Recipe Conversion

The following ingredients and quantities are for a recipe for Noodle Bowl with Stir-Fried Vegetables, yielding 12 portions, 4 oz noodles and 6 oz vegetables each. Convert the recipe to the yields indicated.

	12 portions, 4 oz noodles each 6 oz vegetables each	18 portions, 4 oz noodles each 6 oz vegetables each	18 portions, 5 oz noodles each 8 oz vegetables each
Vegetable oil	2 fl oz		
Scallions	4		
Garlic cloves	2		
Chopped ginger root	1 tsp		
Carrots	6 oz		
Red bell peppers	6 oz		
Shiitake mushroom caps	8 oz		
Bok choy	1 lb		
Mung bean sprouts	4 oz		
Snow peas	8 oz		
Firm tofu	1 lb 4 oz		
Roasted peanuts	6 oz		
Soy sauce	3 fl oz		
Hoisin sauce	2 fl oz		
Vegetable stock	4 fl oz		
Sesame oil	1 tbsp		
Cooked Chinese noodles	3 lb		

D. Recipe Conversion—Metric

The following ingredients and quantities are for a recipe for Noodle Bowl with Stir-Fried Vegetables, yielding 12 portions, 125 g noodles and 180 g vegetables each. Convert the recipe to the yields indicated.

	12 portions, 125 g noodles each 180 g vegetables each	18 portions, 125 g noodles each 180 g vegetables each	18 portions, 150 g noodles each 250 g vegetables each
Vegetable oil	60 mL	_____	_____
Scallions	4	_____	_____
Garlic cloves	2	_____	_____
Chopped ginger root	5 mL	_____	_____
Carrots	180 g	_____	_____
Red bell peppers	180 g	_____	_____
Shiitake mushroom caps	250 g	_____	_____
Bok choy	500 g	_____	_____
Mung bean sprouts	125 g	_____	_____
Snow peas	250 g	_____	_____
Firm tofu	625 g	_____	_____
Roasted peanuts	180 g	_____	_____
Soy sauce	90 mL	_____	_____
Hoisin sauce	60 mL	_____	_____
Vegetable stock	125 mL	_____	_____
Sesame oil	15 mL	_____	_____
Cooked Chinese noodles	1.5 kg	_____	_____

Chapter 21

Salad Dressings and Salads

Although some of the preparations in this chapter involve cooking, most of our attention is on foods that are served and eaten raw. Emphasis is on product understanding and on careful preparation.

After studying Chapter 21, you should be able to:

1. Identify the major salad dressing ingredients.
2. Prepare the following: oil and vinegar dressings, mayonnaise and mayonnaise-based dressings, cooked dressings, and specialty dressings.
3. Identify and describe five different salad types, and select appropriate recipes for use as appetizer, accompaniment, main course, separate course, or dessert salad.
4. Identify a dozen popular salad greens, list six categories of other salad ingredients; and recognize several examples from each category.
5. Judge the quality of fruits and complete the pre-preparation procedures for fruit.
6. Identify the four basic parts of a salad.
7. Prepare and arrange salads that achieve maximum eye appeal.
8. Set up an efficient system for producing salads in quantity.
9. Prepare the following types of salads: green, vegetable, bound, fruit, combination, and gelatin.
10. Set up a successful salad bar and buffet service.

A. Terms

Fill in each blank with the term that is defined or described.

_____ 1. A red-leafed, Italian variety of chickory.

_____ 2. A salad mixed with a heavy dressing, such as mayonnaise, to hold it together.

_____ 3. A famous salad made of romaine lettuce and a dressing made of olive oil, lemon juice, eggs, garlic, and anchovies.

_____ 4. To soak a food in a seasoned liquid to give it flavor and moistness.

_____ 5. A dark brown vinegar that has been aged in wooden barrels.

_____ 6. Oil that has been treated so that it will stay clear and liquid when refrigerated.

_____ 7. A mixture of tender, baby lettuces.

_____ 8. A delicate, tender variety of curly endive that is not as bitter as curly endive.

_____ 9. The best grade of olive oil, made from the first pressing of olives.

_____ 10. A brand of sheep's-milk cheese made only in a specific region of France.

_____ 11. A uniform mixture of two unmixable liquids.

_____ 12. A salad dressing made of oil, vinegar, and seasonings.

_____ 13. Having a smooth scar on the stem end of a melon, with no trace of stem.

_____ 14. A classic salad made of apples, celery, and walnuts, with a mayonnaise-based dressing.

_____ 15. The French name for a small, delicate salad green also known as corn salad, field salad, and lamb's lettuce.

B. True/False

T   F   1. Luncheon salads served as a main course must always contain a meat or seafood item.

T   F   2. The four basic parts of a salad are the underliner, the base, the lettuce, and the garnish.

T   F   3. The dressing should be added to a green salad at least a half hour before service, so that the flavors have time to blend.

T   F   4. Cutting ingredients neatly is one way to enhance the appearance of a salad.

T   F   5. In general, salad ingredients should be in bite-sized pieces.

T   F   6. The purpose of garnish is to make a salad more attractive to the eye.

T   F   7. Peaches, pears, and pineapples are examples of fruits that will discolor when cut and exposed to air.

T   F   **8.** Boston lettuce is often tough and bitter, so it is not used by itself in green salads.

T   F   **9.** Watercress is used mainly as a garnish and is inappropriate in mixed green salads.

T   F   **10.** Moisture is necessary to maintain crispness in salad greens.

T   F   **11.** Cooked vegetables to be used in salads must always be cooked until very tender.

T   F   **12.** Raw ingredients should never be added to bound salads.

T   F   **13.** To prevent food-borne disease, the ingredients of a mayonnaise-based salad must be cold when they are combined.

T   F   **14.** Dressings for fruit salads should never be sweetened, so that they will counteract the sweetness of the fruit.

C. Gelatin Review

1. Gelatin dissolves in water at about _____ degrees Fahrenheit (or _____ degrees Celsius).

2. To avoid lumping, plain gelatin is first mixed with _____.

3. To use a flavored gelatin sweetened with sugar, you need _____ ounces of gelatin mix per gallon of water

   (or _____ grams of gelatin mix per liter of water).

4. Basic proportions for unflavored gelatin are _____ ounces of dry gelatin per gallon of liquid (or _____ grams per liter).

5. The setting power of gelatin is weakened by _____, by _____,

   and by _____. Therefore, most gelatin salads need more

   gelatin than the basic proportion indicated in number 4.

6. To dissolve sweetened, flavored gelatin, stir it into _____ water.

7. _____ and _____ are two examples of fresh fruits that should not be added to gelatin.

8. The proper time to mix solid ingredients into gelatin is _____

   _____.

9. In the space below, write out the basic procedure for unmolding gelatin.

   _____

   _____

   _____

   _____

_____

_____

_____

_____

D. Salad Dressing Review

1. The two main ingredients of most standard salad dressings are _____ and _____ .
   Other ingredients, such as seasonings, herbs, and egg yolks, are added to modify flavor and texture.

2. _____ is an all-purpose blend of oils that can be used for a wide
   variety of dressings because of its neutral flavor.

3. Five examples of different vinegars that can be used to make salad dressings are:

   _____

   _____

   _____

   _____

   _____

4. To make a basic oil and vinegar dressing, you need _____ pint(s) of oil for each pint of vinegar.

5. The most important thickening agent in cooked dressing is _____, while the ingredient that

   makes mayonnaise thick is _____ .

6. So that the dressing will not be too acidic, a vinegar that contains more than 5% acid may have to be

   _____ before being included in the dressing.

7. Suggest one ingredient that can be substituted for oil to make a low-fat vinaigrette. _____

8. In the space below, explain how to make mayonnaise. Be sure to include all necessary steps, and number the
   steps to make the procedure easier to read. Include ingredient quantities if your instructor asks you to do so.

   _____

   _____

   _____

   _____

E. Math Exercise: Trimming Loss

The exercises below are of two kinds, calculating yield and calculating amount needed. To do the calculations, you need to know the percentage yield for each fruit, as listed in Chapter 21 of the text. For your convenience, the necessary percentages are repeated here.

Apples	75%	Papayas	65%
Bananas	70%	Peaches	75%
Kiwi fruit	80%	Pears	75%
Mangoes	75%	Pineapples	50%
Oranges (sectioned)	65%	Watermelon	45%

Calculating Amount Needed

Assume you need the following quantities, EP (edible portion, with no peels, pits, cores, or stems), of the indicated fresh fruits. Calculate the AP weight you will need to get the required yield. (Questions 1–7 use U.S. measures; questions 8–14 use metric measures. Answer whichever questions are assigned by your instructor.)

	EP Weight Desired	AP Weight Needed
1. Bananas	12 oz	_____
2. Apples	2 lb	_____
3. Peaches	3 lb	_____
4. Oranges (sectioned)	½ lb	_____
5. Kiwi fruit	6 oz	_____
6. Pineapple	8 oz	_____
7. Papaya	1½ lb	_____
8. Bananas	350 g	_____
9. Apples	1 kg	_____
10. Peaches	1.5 kg	_____
11. Oranges (sections)	250 g	_____
12. Kiwi fruit	175 g	_____
13. Pineapple	250 g	_____
14. Papaya	750 g	_____

Calculating Yield

Assume you have the following quantities, AP, of the indicated fresh fruits. Calculate the EP weight you will have left after trimming, peeling, coring, etc. (Questions 15–21 use U.S. measures; questions 22–28 use metric measures. Answer whichever questions are assigned by your instructor.)

	AP Weight	EP Weight
15. Pears	3½ lb	_____
16. Bananas	6 lb	_____
17. Mangoes	2½ lb	_____
18. Watermelon	4½ lb	_____
19. Kiwi fruit	1 lb	_____
20. Apples	2 lb	_____
21. Pineapple	3½ lb	_____
22. Pears	1.6 kg	_____
23. Bananas	3 kg	_____
24. Mangoes	1.2 kg	_____
25. Watermelon	2.3 kg	_____
26. Kiwi fruit	400 g	_____
27. Apples	1 kg	_____
28. Pineapple	1.5 kg	_____

F. Recipe Conversion

The following ingredients and quantities are for a recipe for Cucumbers and Onions in Sour Cream, yielding 25 salads at 3½ oz each. Convert the recipe to the yields indicated.

	25 portions, 3½ oz each	40 portions, 3½ oz each	14 portions, 3 oz each
Cider vinegar	1 pt	_____	_____
Water	1 cup	_____	_____
Sugar	1 oz	_____	_____
Salt	2 tsp	_____	_____
White pepper	½ tsp	_____	_____
Cucumbers, peeled	4 lb	_____	_____
Onions, peeled	1 lb	_____	_____
Sour cream	1 pt	_____	_____
Mayonnaise	1 cup	_____	_____
Lettuce leaves for underliners*	25	_____	_____

Note: This ingredient is calculated differently from the others. Can you see why?

Recipe Conversion—Metric

The following ingredients and quantities are for a recipe for Cucumbers and Onions in Sour Cream, yielding 25 salads at 100 g each. Convert the recipe to the yields indicated.

	25 portions, 100 g each	40 portions, 100 g each	14 portions, 90 g each
Cider vinegar	500 mL	_____	_____
Water	250 mL	_____	_____
Sugar	30 g	_____	_____
Salt	10 mL	_____	_____
White pepper	2 mL	_____	_____
Cucumbers, peeled	2 kg	_____	_____
Onions, peeled	500 g	_____	_____
Sour cream	500 mL	_____	_____
Mayonnaise	250 mL	_____	_____
Lettuce leaves for underliners*	25	_____	_____

*Note: This ingredient is calculated differently from the others. Can you see why?

G. Portion Cost

Cost out the following recipe. For prices of the ingredients, use figures supplied by your instructor or the *Sample Prices* in the Appendix of this *Study Guide*.

ITEM: **CARROT RAISIN SALAD**

Ingredient	Recipe Quantity	AP Quantity	Price	Total Amount
Carrots, AP	5 lb	_____	_____	_____
Raisins	8 oz	_____	_____	_____
Mayonnaise	1½ cups	_____	_____	_____
Salad oil	6 fl oz	_____	_____	_____
Wine vinegar	2 fl oz	_____	_____	_____
Iceberg lettuce	1 head	_____	_____	_____

Total cost _____

Number of portions   25

Cost per portion _____

Portion Cost—Metric

Cost out the following recipe. For prices of the ingredients, use figures supplied by your instructor or the *Sample Prices* in the Appendix of this *Study Guide*.

ITEM: **CARROT RAISIN SALAD**

Ingredient	Recipe Quantity	AP Quantity	Price	Total Amount
Carrots, AP	2 kg	_____	_____	_____
Raisins	200 g	_____	_____	_____
Mayonnaise	300 mL	_____	_____	_____
Salad oil	150 mL	_____	_____	_____
Wine vinegar	50 mL	_____	_____	_____
Iceberg lettuce	1 head	_____	_____	_____
			Total cost	_____
			Number of portions	25
			Cost per portion	_____

Chapter 22

Sandwiches

Chapters 22 through 27 are a continuation of the pantry unit begun in Chapter 21. This chapter covers the basics of preparing sandwiches of all types. Although sandwich production may seem simple at first glance, it exemplifies many of the basic principles of the professional kitchen, such as careful and thorough mise en place, well-developed manual skills, and efficient planning and organization of tasks.

After studying Chapter 22, you should be able to:

1. Select, store, and serve fresh, good-quality breads for sandwiches.
2. Use sandwich spreads correctly.
3. Identify the most popular types of sandwich fillings.
4. Set up an efficient sandwich station.
5. Prepare the major types of sandwiches to order.
6. Prepare sandwiches in quantity.

A. Terms

Fill in each blank with the term that is defined or described.

Reuban **1.** A sandwich made of corned beef, sauerkraut, Swiss cheese, and Russian dressing on rye bread.

Pullman Loaf **2.** A long, rectangular loaf of bread, often used for sandwiches.

Simple Cold/hot Sandwich **3.** A sandwich that consists of a filling between two slices of bread.

Open-faced Sandwich **4.** A sandwich made of a slice of bread with a topping, but with no top slice of bread.

Club Sandwich **5.** A multidecker sandwich made of three slices of toast spread with mayonnaise and filled with sliced chicken or turkey, lettuce, tomato, and bacon.

Tea Sandwich **6.** A small, fancy sandwich, generally made from light, delicate ingredients and bread that has been trimmed of crusts.

Pizza **7.** A thin sheet of bread dough baked with a topping, often but not always including tomatoes and cheese.

Wrap **8.** A cold sandwich in which the filling is wrapped in a tortilla or similar thin dough product.

eggplant, roasted pepper, and Fontina Panino **9.** A hot grilled sandwich usually prepared in equipment that compresses the bread _in a press_ and filling and grills both sides of the sandwich at the same time.

B. Short-Answer Questions

1. List six types of bread that can be used for sandwiches.

(a) _Rye_

(b) _Wheat_

(c) _Pumpernickel_

(d) _Multigrain_

(e) _Kaiser_

(f) _Ciabatta_

2. What are the two most commonly used spreads for sandwiches?

Butter

Mayonnaise

3. The following are some basic categories of sandwich filling ingredients. Fill in the blanks with specific examples of each group, naming as many examples as there are spaces.

Beef

(a) _Sliced roast beef (hot or cold)_

(b) _Hamburger patties_

(c) _Small steaks_

(d) _Corned beef_

(e) _Pastrami_

(f) _Tongue, fresh or smoked_

Pork and sausage products

(a) _Roast Pork_

(b) _BBQ pork_

(c) _Ham_

(d) _bacon_

(e) _Canadian bacon_

(f) _Salami_

(g) _Bologna_

Poultry

(a) _turkey breast_

(b) _Chicken breast_

Fish and shellfish

(a) _tuna_

(b) _Sardines_

(c) _Shrimp_

(d) _anchovies_

Cheese

(a) _____ Cheddar _____

(b) _____ Swiss _____

(c) _____ provolone _____

(d) _____ Cream Cheese _____

(e) _____ Cheese spreads _____

4. List four basic hand tools that are essential on a short-order sandwich station.

(a) _____ Spatulas _____

(b) _____ Knives _____

(c) _____ Cutting board _____

(d) _____ power slicer _____

5. In the space below, draw a diagram of the proper way to cut a club sandwich.

6. Suppose you are assigned to make a large quantity of turkey sandwiches, using mayonnaise as the spread and lettuce leaves and sliced turkey breast as the filling. In the space below, write out the procedure you would use to prepare the sandwiches efficiently and quickly. Be sure to include all the steps, and number the steps to make the procedure easier to read.

7. Two of the most basic and classic Italian pizzas are called Margherita and Marinara. List the toppings for these two pizzas.

Margherita: _plum tomatoes, basil leaves, mozzarella, parmesan_

Marinara: _tomatoes (plum), oregano_

8. What technique is used to make a grilled panino sandwich if a panino press is not available?

Use a griddle and place grill brick on sandwich same for both sides

C. Recipe Conversion

The following ingredients and quantities are for Chili Marinade for Grilled Salmon Sandwiches. Convert the recipe to the yields indicated.

	6 oz	16 oz	40 oz
Chili powder	2 oz	5.5 oz	
Dried oregano	1 tbsp		
Ground cloves	½ tsp		
Garlic, crushed	1 oz		
Salt	2 tsp		
Brown sugar	1 oz		
Red wine vinegar	4 fl oz		

Recipe Conversion—Metric

The following ingredients and quantities are for Chili Marinade for Grilled Salmon Sandwiches. Convert the recipe to the yields indicated.

	180	500 g	1.25 kg
Chili powder	60 g	_____	_____
Dried oregano	15 mL	_____	_____
Ground cloves	2 mL	_____	_____
Garlic, crushed	30 g	_____	_____
Salt	10 mL	_____	_____
Brown sugar	30 g	_____	_____
Red wine vinegar	120 mL	_____	_____

Chapter 23

Hors d'Oeuvres

Because there are so many kinds of hors d'oeuvres, using all types of meats, poultry, fish, vegetables, and starch products, in this chapter you will use all the skills you have learned in earlier chapters.

After studying Chapter 23, you should be able to:

1. Name and describe the two principal methods of serving hors d'oeuvres at a reception.
2. Prepare canapés.
3. Prepare hors d'oeuvres cocktails and relishes.
4. Prepare dips.
5. Prepare a variety of other hors d'oeuvres, including antipasti, bruschette, and tapas.
6. Name and describe the three types of sturgeon caviar, and name and describe three other kinds of caviar.

A. Terms

Fill in each blank with the term that is defined or described.

___Canapés___   **1.** A bite-sized, open-faced sandwich, served as an hors d'oeuvre.

___Crudités___   **2.** French term for raw vegetables, served as hors d'oeuvres.

___relish___   **3.** A category of hors d'oeuvres that includes raw vegetables (as in number 2) and pickled items.

___Guacamole___   **4.** A Mexican-style dip made of mashed avocado.

___Cocktail___   **5.** A category of appetizer that includes various seafoods or fruits, served cold, usually with a tart or tangy sauce.

___antipasto___   **6.** An Italian hors d'oeuvre.

amuse bouche   **7.** A small appetizer offered, compliments of the chef, to guests seated at their tables, either before or after they have ordered from the menu.

bruschetta   **8.** Italian-style garlic toast, usually served with toppings. Similar to large canapés.

Caviar   **9.** Salted sturgeon eggs.

tapa   **10.** Spanish-style hors d'oeuvre, usually served on a small plate and intended to be eaten with wine or other drinks.

B. Hors d'Oeuvre Review

1. The three basic parts of a canapé are *Base* , *Spread* , and *Garnish* .

2. In the space below, draw diagrams of three different ways that bread slices can be cut into various shapes for canapés.

3. List four different items that can be used as bases for canapés.

   (a) *Bread/Toast*
   (b) *Mini Pancakes*
   (c) *tiny unsweetened pastry shells*
   (d) *tortilla chips/crackers*

4. What are the two most common types of spreads used for canapés?

   butter

   Softened *Cream Cheese*

5. The following are some basic categories of canapé garnishes. Fill in the blanks with specific examples of each group, naming as many examples as there are spaces.

Fish and shellfish products

(a) crab meat

(b) Smoked oysters + clams

(c) Smoked salmon

(d) Herring

(e) Shrimp

(f) Sardines

(g) Smoked trout

(h) lobster chunks

Vegetables, pickles, and relishes

(a) radish slices

(b) olives

(c) pickles

(d) capers

(e) pimento

(f) pickled onions

(g) Chutney

(h) Parsley

(i) Marinated mushrooms

(j) Cucumber slices

Meats

(a) ham

(b) Salami

(c) Chicken or turkey breast

(d) Roast beef

6. The two primary methods of serving hors d'oeuvres are ___Hot___ and ___Cold___ .

7. When raw oysters are served as a seafood cocktail, the best way to keep them cold is _____

_in a bed of ice_____ .

8. When hot items are served on an hors d'oeuvre buffet, the best way to keep them hot is _____

_Serve in a Chafing dish_____ .

9. Describe the proper consistency for dips. _thick, but not so thick where_____

_a chip will break_____

_____

10. Describe the procedure for making a basic bruschetta. _toast bread on grill or_____

broiler, rub one side of each piece with cut

clove of garlic while still hot, brush or drizzel

olive oil so toast is partially soaked, salt &

pepper to taste

11. The three categories of caviar, ranging from the largest to the smallest, are _Salmon Caviar_ ,

Black Roe , and _tobiko_ .

12. Caviar made with a relatively low proportion of salt is called _Malassol_ .

13. Proper serving temperature for caviar is _ice cold_ .

C. Recipe Conversion

The following ingredients and quantities are for a Clam Dip recipe that yields 1 qt. Convert the recipe to the yields indicated.

	1 qt	1½ pt	1 gal
Cream cheese	1 lb 4 oz	_____	_____
Clam juice	3 oz	_____	_____
Dijon-style mustard	2 oz	_____	_____
Worcestershire sauce	1 oz	_____	_____
Horseradish	1 tsp	_____	_____
Grated onion	1½ oz	_____	_____
Hot pepper sauce	½ tsp	_____	_____
Canned clams, drained	12 oz	_____	_____
Salt	to taste	_____	_____
White pepper	to taste	_____	_____

Recipe Conversion—Metric

The following ingredients and quantities are for a Clam Dip recipe that yields 1 L. Convert the recipe to the yields indicated.

	1 L	750 mL	4 L
Cream cheese	625 g	_____	_____
Clam juice	90 g	_____	_____
Dijon-style mustard	60 g	_____	_____
Worcestershire sauce	30 mL	_____	_____
Horseradish	5 mL	_____	_____
Grated onion	45 g	_____	_____
Hot pepper sauce	2 ml	_____	_____
Canned clams, drained	375 g	_____	_____
Salt	to taste	_____	_____
White pepper	to taste	_____	_____

Chapter 24

Breakfast Preparation

This chapter discusses cooking techniques for breakfast items, illustrated by a few typical recipes. In addition, there is important product information about eggs.

After studying Chapter 24, you should be able to:

1. Describe the composition of eggs and the major differences among grades.

2. Store eggs properly.

3. Prepare the following egg items: hard-, medium-, and soft-cooked eggs; poached eggs; fried eggs; baked eggs; scrambled eggs; omelets; entrée soufflés; and savory custards.

4. List the key differences between waffle batter and pancake batter, and prepare each.

5. Prepare French toast, and identify the common variations possible by changing the basic ingredients.

6. Prepare each of the two general types of cooked breakfast cereals.

7. Identify the three most common breakfast meats and prepare them.

A. Terms

Fill in each blank with the term that is defined or described.

_____ 1. A dish consisting of poached eggs and Canadian bacon on English muffins, coated with Hollandaise sauce.

sunny side up 2. Term used to describe fried eggs cooked on one side only.

shirred 3. An egg baked in an individual serving dish, with or without additional ingredients; resembles a fried egg in appearance.

fritta 4. A flat, unfolded omelet, consisting of beaten eggs mixed with other ingredients.

quiche 5. A savory tart consisting of a custard mixture and other ingredients baked in a pastry shell.

french toast   6. Bread dipped into an egg mixture and cooked on a griddle or in a fry pan or deep-fryer.

custard   7. A liquid that is thickened or set by the coagulation of egg protein.

crepe   8. A thin pancake made without any leavening.

salmonella   9. A food-borne disease that may be spread by contaminated eggs.

B. True/False: Egg and Breakfast Review

(T) F   1. Fresh or high-grade raw eggs are firmer (less runny) than old or low-grade eggs.

(T) F   2. The highest government grade for fresh eggs is grade AAA.

(T) F   3. One extra-large shell egg weighs slightly more than 2 oz (including the shell).

(T) F   4. Egg yolks are high in fat.

(T) F   5. The green color sometimes seen in eggs is due to overcooking.

T (F)   6. A custard mixture must be heated to the boiling point of water (212°F/100°C) so that it will set properly.   _185°F no higher_

T (F)   7. Egg whites whip better and make a richer foam if the bowl is lightly greased before breaking the eggs into it.

T (F)   8. Hard-cooked eggs will be tough and rubbery unless they are cooked long enough to be tenderized.   _low enough heat for enough time_

T (F)   9. To make soft-cooked eggs, shell eggs are boiled for 5 to 7 minutes.   _1 minute_

T (F)   10. The air sac is located at the small end of the egg.

(T) F   11. A pinch of cream of tartar improves the foaming ability of egg whites.

(T) F   12. Making a true French omelet requires high heat.

(T) F   13. A standard spinach soufflé is made from a thick white sauce, egg yolks, chopped cooked spinach (and sometimes other ingredients for flavoring), plus whipped egg whites folded in just before baking.

T (F)   14. Waffle batter is usually thinner than pancake batter.

T F   15. Pancake batter should be beaten well to develop a smooth texture.

T (F)   16. The best way to prepare a large quantity of bacon is to cook it in the deep-fryer.   _oven_

T (F)   17. Egg substitutes used for making scrambled eggs contain real egg whites but not yolks.

(T) F   18. Egg shells are porous, so whole shell eggs can absorb foreign odors when in storage.

(T) F   19. Sugar whipped into egg whites make an egg white foam more stable.

C. Recipe Conversion

The following ingredients and quantities are for a vegetable frittata recipe that yields 4 portions at 8 oz each. Convert the recipe to the yields indicated.

	4 portions, 8 oz each	10 portions, 8 oz each	10 portions, 6 oz each
Leeks	4 oz	_____	_____
Zucchini	10 oz	_____	_____
Butter	1½ oz	_____	_____
Spinach leaves	8 oz	_____	_____
Eggs, beaten	10 fl oz	_____	_____

Recipe Conversion—Metric

The following ingredients and quantities are a vegetable frittata recipe that yields 4 portions at 240 g each. Convert the recipe to the yields indicated.

	4 portions, 240 g each	10 portions, 240 g each	10 portions, 180 g each
Leeks	4 oz	_____	_____
Zucchini	10 oz	_____	_____
Butter	1½ oz	_____	_____
Spinach leaves	8 oz	_____	_____
Eggs, beaten	10 fl oz	_____	_____

Chapter 25

Dairy and Beverages

Much of this chapter consists of important product information. Here you learn to identify the major types of milk, cream, butter, and cheese products and to cook with them using proper techniques. In addition, you learn about the preparation of coffee and tea beverages.

After studying Chapter 25, you should be able to:

1. Describe the major milk, cream, and butter products.
2. Explain why milk curdles and why it scorches, and identify the steps to take to prevent curdling and scorching.
3. Whip cream.
4. Describe the most important kinds of cheese used in the kitchen.
5. Store and serve cheese properly.
6. Cook with cheese.
7. Prepare coffee and tea.

A. Terms

Fill in each blank with the term that is defined or described.

Homogenized   1. Milk that has been processed so that the cream doesn't separate out.

Chèvre   2. Generic term for cheese made with goats' milk.

Magarine   3. A manufactured product made of fats and other ingredients, intended to resemble butter.

Welsh Rabbit   4. A dish made of cheddar-type cheese melted with beer and seasonings.

pasteurized   5. Milk that has been heat-treated to kill disease-causing bacteria.

raw milk   6. Milk that has not been heat-treated as in number 5.

curdle   7. A process by which milk proteins coagulate and separate from the whey; in cooking this process is usually undesirable.

espresso   8. A strong, dark coffee made from beans roasted until they are almost black.

Black tea   9. Tea that has been fermented by allowing the freshly harvested leaves to oxidize in a damp place.

Green tea   10. Tea that has been dried without the fermenting procedure described in number 9.

Oolong   11. Tea that has been only partially fermented, so that it has a greenish-brown color.

expresso   12. A term meaning "half-cup," referring to strong, dark coffee served in small cups after dinner.

Swiss fondue   13. A dish consisting of Swiss cheeses melted with white wine and served with bread cubes for dipping.

crème fraîche   14. A slightly aged, cultured heavy cream, often used for sauce-making.

farm   15. Cheese that is made with milk from the farmer's own herd or flock on the farm where the animals are raised.

Artisan   16. Cheese that is produced primarily by hand, in small batches, with particular attention to the cheesemaker's art and using as little mechanization as possible.

Cappuccino   17. A drink made of equal parts espresso and frothy, steamed milk.

Mocha   18. A drink made of espresso and hot chocolate or cocoa.

latte   19. A drink made of espresso and steamed milk, using at least twice as much milk as coffee.

Chai   20. A sweetened blend of tea and hot, spiced milk.

B. Dairy and Cheese Review I

1. In the blanks provided, write in the name of the milk or cream products described.

   (a) _buttermilk_ Fresh, liquid, skim milk that has been cultured by bacteria.

   (b) _Condensed_ Milk that has had about 60% of its water content removed.

   (c) _dried whole milk_ Skim milk that has been dried to a powder.

   (d) _whole milk_ Milk produced by disease-free herds under strict sanitary conditions.

   (e) _raw milk_ Milk that has not been pasteurized.

   (f) _Sour cream_ Cream that has been fermented by certain bacteria to make it thick.

   (g) _____ Sweetened milk with more than half its moisture removed.

   (h) _Skim/nonfat_ Milk with all or nearly all its fat removed.

   (i) _fortified_ Milk with added vitamins.

   (j) _Ultra high temp_ _Pasturization or ultra pasturized_ Milk that has been processed at a higher temperature to make it shelf-stable until opened.

2. In the blanks provided, write in the fat content (in percent) of each of the following milk and cream products.

   (a) _30-40_ % Heavy whipping cream

   (b) _3.5_ % Whole milk

   (c) _10-18_ % Half-and-half

   (d) _5 or less_ % Skim milk

   (e) _82_ % Butter

   (f) _30-35_ % Light cream

3. What is yogurt? _milk cultured by special bacteria and having a custard like consistancy_

4. Name four conditions or substances that can make milk curdle.

   (a) _reconstituted dry milk_

   (b) _reduce temps & time_

   (c) _Salt lightly_

   (d) _Use starches_

5. In order to be in the best condition for whipping, heavy cream should be at about what temperature?

Chilled

6. Describe the appearance of properly whipped cream. What happens if the cream is whipped too much?

It has stiff peaks, and if done too much
it turns into butter

7. What is the highest government grade of butter? _AA_

8. What does the term "ripen" mean when referring to cheese?

a process that converts freshly made curd into
distinctive, flavorful cheese

9. Cheeses can be classified according to how and if they are ripened. List the five categories, and give an example of each kind of cheese.

(a) _Bacteria ripened from inside_   Example: _Cheddar, swiss, gouda, parmesan_

(b) _Washed-rind cheeses_   Example: _limberger, liederkranz_

(c) _Blue-veined cheeses_   Example: _Roquefort, stilton_

(d) _Mold-rind cheeses_   Example: _Brie, Camembert, St. Andre_

(e) _Unripened cheeses_   Example: _Cottage, cream, baker's_

10. The label on a package of soft cheese indicates a net weight of 8 oz (227 g) and a fat content of 75%. What is the total weight of the fat in the cheese? Explain your answer. (Caution: This may be a trick question.)

11. What is the proper serving temperature for most cheeses?

room temperature

C. Cheese Review II

The left column below lists the names of various cheeses. The column on the right lists various categories or kinds of cheese. In the space before the name of each cheese, write the letter corresponding to the kind of cheese it is.

d	**1.** Cheddar	**a.** Unripened
e	**2.** Roquefort	**b.** Semisoft
f	**3.** Boucheron	**c.** Soft ripened
c	**4.** Brie	**d.** Hard ripened
c	**5.** Limburger	**e.** Blue-veined
d	**6.** Parmesan	**f.** Goat cheese
d	**7.** Emmenthaler	**g.** Hard grating (grana)
h	**8.** American	**h.** Process
e	**9.** Stilton
b	**10.** Port Salut
a	**11.** Mozzarella
e	**12.** Gorgonzola
g	**13.** Romano
d	**14.** Fontina
a	**15.** Ricotta
c	**16.** Liederkranz
a	**17.** Cottage
c	**18.** Camembert
	19. Bel Paese
f	**20.** Montrachet

D. Recipe Conversion

The following ingredients and quantities are for a Welsh Rabbit recipe that yields 25 portions at 4 oz each. Convert the recipe to the yields indicated.

	25 portions, 4 oz each	4 portions, 4 oz each	16 portions, 3 oz each
Worcestershire sauce	3 tbsp	_____	_____
Dry mustard	2 tsp	_____	_____
Cayenne	pinch	_____	_____
Beer	2½ cups	_____	_____
Cheddar cheese	5 lb	_____	_____
White bread*	25 slices	_____	_____

*Note: This ingredient is calculated differently from the others.

Recipe Conversion—Metric

The following ingredients and quantities are for a Welsh Rabbit recipe that yields 25 portions at 125 g each. Convert the recipe to the yields indicated.

	25 portions, 125 g each	4 portions, 125 g each	16 portions, 100 g each
Worcestershire sauce	45 mL	_____	_____
Dry mustard	10 mL	_____	_____
Cayenne	pinch	_____	_____
Beer	625 mL	_____	_____
Cheddar cheese	2.5 kg	_____	_____
White bread*	25 slices	_____	_____

*Note: This ingredient is calculated differently from the others.

E. Portion Cost

Cost out the following recipe. For prices of the ingredients, use figures supplied by your instructor or the *Sample Prices* in the Appendix of this *Study Guide*.

ITEM: **CHEESE TART**

Ingredient	Recipe Quantity	AP Quantity	Price	Total Amount
Flour	2 lb	_____	_____	_____
Shortening	1 lb 4 oz	_____	_____	_____
Salt	1½ oz	_____	_____	_____
Water	8 oz	_____	_____	_____
Gruyère cheese	2 lb	_____	_____	_____
Eggs	24	_____	_____	_____
Heavy cream	1 qt	_____	_____	_____
Milk	2 qt	_____	_____	_____
Salt	½ oz	_____	_____	_____

Total cost _____

Number of portions   48

Cost per portion _____

Portion Cost—Metric

Cost out the following recipe. For prices of the ingredients, use figures supplied by your instructor or the *Sample Prices* in the Appendix of this *Study Guide*.

ITEM: **CHEESE TART**

Ingredient	Recipe Quantity	AP Quantity	Price	Total Amount
Flour	1 kg	_____	_____	_____
Shortening	625 g	_____	_____	_____
Salt	15 g	_____	_____	_____
Water	250 mL	_____	_____	_____
Gruyère cheese	1 kg	_____	_____	_____
Eggs	24	_____	_____	_____
Heavy cream	1 L	_____	_____	_____
Milk	2 L	_____	_____	_____
Salt	15 g	_____	_____	_____

Total cost _____

Number of portions   48

Cost per portion _____

Chapter 26

Sausages and Cured Foods

This chapter introduces the specialized subjects of curing, smoking, and sausage-making. This material is part of the general study of garde manger, which you first read about in Chapter 21, Salad Dressings and Salads. There is a great deal of technical information in this chapter, much of which affects food safety, so it is important to study it thoroughly before producing any of the recipes here.

After studying Chapter 26, you should be able to:

1. Prepare simple dry-cured and brine-cured foods.
2. Prepare simple smoked foods.
3. Prepare fresh, cured, and smoked sausages.

A. Terms

Fill in each blank with the term that is defined or described.

_____ 1. A curing method in which the curing ingredients are packed or rubbed over the food.

_____ 2. A curing method in which the food is immersed in a solution of the curing ingredients dissolved in water.

_____ 3. A spice mixture used in some sausages and other meat products. The name means "4 spices."

_____ 4. A sausage that contains no nitrates or nitrites.

_____ 5. An artificial but edible sausage casing made of animal connective tissue.

_____ 6. A smoking method in which the foods are smoked at a high enough temperature to cook them partially or completely.

_____ 7. The curing agent or chemical in Prague Powder #1, or curing salt.

_____ **8.** A cancer-causing chemical formed when meat containing nitrates is subjected to very high heat.

_____ **9.** A sausage grind in which the meat and fat are ground very smooth with the addition of ice or water.

_____ **10.** The art of making prepared and cooked meat products, especially pork products such as sausages and pâtés.

_____ **11.** A sausage casing made from animal intestine.

_____ **12.** A medium-sized casing, about 1 to 1½ inches (3 to 4 cm) in diameter, used for such popular sausages as bratwurst and Italian sausage.

_____ **13.** A smoking method in which the temperature is kept low so that the smoked food remains uncooked.

_____ **14.** A patty of sausage meat wrapped in caul.

B. Review of Curing and Smoking

1. The most important ingredient for curing any food, including cured fish, is _____ . This ingredient has two main effects, both of which make the food less hospitable to bacteria:

   (a) _____

   _____ and

   (b) _____

   _____ .

2. Curing salt consists of _____ and _____, plus coloring to give it

   a _____ color. The purpose of the coloring agent is _____ .

3. Two other names for curing salt are _____ and _____ .

4. The two basic types of cures are _____ and _____ .

5. Of the two types of cures in question 4, which is most often used for curing whole poultry? _____

6. What is the main reason for curing all meats, poultry, and fish before smoking them?

   _____

   _____

   _____

7. When cold-smoking food, you should keep the temperature inside the smokehouse to _____ or lower.

8. A smokehouse consists of four main elements:

a. _____

b. _____

c. _____

d. _____

9. The smoking process consists of three main steps:

a. _____

b. _____

c. _____

C. Review of Sausage-Making

1. The four basic components of fresh sausage meat are _____ , _____ ,

_____ , and _____ .

2. When extra fat must be added to pork sausage meat, what is the most desirable fat to use? _____

3. To increase the moisture content of low-fat sausage, you can add _____ because they help

retain moisture.

4. Describe how to prepare natural sausage casings for stuffing.

_____

_____

_____

_____

_____

_____

5. The two basic types of grinds used in the production of sausages are _____ and

_____ . Briefly describe the differences between these two grinding procedures.

_____

_____

_____

_____

_____

_____

_____

6. Why must sausage meat be kept very cold during grinding and stuffing?

_____

_____

D. Recipe Conversion

The following ingredients and quantities are for an Italian sausage recipe that yields 6 lb. Convert the recipe to the yields indicated.

	6 lb	2 lb	15 lb
Lean pork	4 lb 8 oz	_____	_____
Pork fatback	1 lb 8 oz	_____	_____
Salt	2 tbsp	_____	_____
Black pepper	2 tsp	_____	_____
Fennel seeds	1 tbsp	_____	_____
Paprika	5 tsp	_____	_____
Crushed red pepper	1 tsp	_____	_____
Sugar	2 tsp	_____	_____
Cold water	6 oz	_____	_____

E. Recipe Conversion—Metric

The following ingredients and quantities are for an Italian sausage recipe that yields 3 kg. Convert the recipe to the yields indicated.

	3 kg	1 kg	7.5 kg
Lean pork	2250 g	_____	_____
Pork fatback	750 g	_____	_____
Salt	30 g	_____	_____
Black pepper	10 mL	_____	_____
Fennel seeds	15 mL	_____	_____
Paprika	25 mL	_____	_____
Crushed red pepper	5 mL	_____	_____
Sugar	10 mL	_____	_____
Cold water	200 mL	_____	_____

Chapter 27

Pâtés, Terrines, and Other Cold Foods

Your study of garde manger continues with an introduction to the production of pâtés and terrines. These products are not only some of the most important items on the classic cold buffet (which you will read more about in Chapter 28), but they are also served as appetizers on restaurant menus.

After studying Chapter 27, you should be able to:

1. Prepare and use aspic jellies.
2. Prepare and use classic chaud-froid and mayonnaise chaud-froid.
3. Prepare livers for use in forcemeats.
4. Prepare basic meat and poultry forcemeats.
5. Prepare pâtés and terrines using basic forcemeats.
6. Prepare galantines.
7. Prepare mousseline forcemeats and make terrines based on them.
8. Prepare specialty terrines and other molded dishes based on aspics and mousses.
9. Handle raw foie gras and prepare foie gras terrines.
10. Prepare baked liver terrines.
11. Prepare rillettes.

A. Terms

Fill in each blank with the term that is defined or described.

_____ **1.** Liver of specially fattened ducks and geese.

_____ **2.** A forcemeat made of puréed meat, poultry, or fish, heavy cream, and, usually, egg whites.

_____   **3.** The department of a kitchen in which cold foods, including salads and buffet items, are prepared.

_____   **4.** A clarified stock that contains enough gelatin so that it solidifies when cold.

_____   **5.** Unflavored gelatin mixed with a powdered stock base.

_____   **6.** A seasoned mixture of ground meats and other foods, used as a filling or stuffing or as a base for terrines and pâtés.

_____   **7.** Dough or pastry used to make pâtés.

_____   **8.** An opaque, usually white, sauce containing gelatin, used to coat certain cold foods for decorative purposes.

_____   **9.** A seasoned mixture of cooked meat and fat, mashed to a paste; used as an appetizer.

_____   **10.** A creamy, puréed food made light by the addition of whipped cream; often contains gelatin.

_____   **11.** A dish made of a baked forcemeat, usually in a crust.

_____   **12.** A dish similar to that described in number 11, except made without a crust; traditionally baked in an earthenware mold.

_____   **13.** A special type of the item described in number 11, characterized by a coarse texture.

_____   **14.** A forcemeat wrapped in the skin of the animal from which it is made, such as chicken or duck, or rolled into a cylinder without the skin.

B. Review of Aspic and Chaud-Froid Procedures

1. In the space below, write the three basic steps for making a classic aspic jelly.

_____

_____

_____

_____

_____

_____

2. In the space below, write the steps in the general procedure for making a cooled, liquid aspic jelly for coating a food item. Start with cold, solidified aspic jelly.

_____

_____

_____

_____

_____

_____

3. In the space below, write the steps in the general procedure for coating foods with aspic jelly.

_____

_____

_____

_____

_____

_____

4. In the space below, write the ingredients and the procedure for making mayonnaise chaud-froid.

_____

_____

_____

_____

_____

5. In the space below, write the procedure for coating a mold with a uniform layer of aspic jelly.

_____

_____

_____

_____

_____

_____

C. Short-Answer Questions

1. It is especially important to be aware of safe, sanitary food handling when preparing cold foods such as

   pâtés because _____

   _____

   _____

   _____ .

2. The procedure for making a classic aspic jelly is similar to the procedure for making what kind of soup?

   _____

3. Three ingredients that can be included with the regular bones when making stock to help increase the gelatin

   content are _____ , _____ , and _____ .

4. Mayonnaise chaud-froid is made from two ingredients, _____

   and _____ .

5. Classical chaud-froid can be made by adding a liaison to _____ .

6. Three examples of classic pâté garnish are _____ , _____ , and

   _____ .

7. A gratin forcemeat is similar to a straight forcemeat, except that some of the meat is _____ .

   This type of forcemeat contains a starch binder called a _____ .

8. In addition to pork and pork fat, a country-style forcemeat usually contains some _____ .

9. Basic-grind sausage meat is similar to which of the three basic forcemeat types discussed in this chapter?

   _____

10. The most important meat used in the production of pâtés and terrines is _____ .

11. A basic straight forcemeat is made of _____ percent meat and _____

    percent fat.

12. In five steps, write the procedure for preparing poultry livers for use in forcemeats.

a. _____

b. _____

c. _____

d. _____

e. _____

13. In simplest terms, a terrine is a baked _____.

14. After a pâté en croûte has baked and cooled, the next step is to pour _____ through the steam vent holes in order to fill up the space between the crust and the forcemeat, which has shrunk during baking.

15. A mousseline forcemeat is made of puréed meat, poultry, or fish, _____, and usually egg whites.

16. The four basic steps in making a savory mousse are:

a. _____

b. _____

c. _____

d. _____

17. A raw foie gras should be at what temperature before being deveined? _____ .

18. When cooking foie gras, it is very important to avoid overcooking because _____

_____

_____ .

Chapter 28

Food Presentation and Garnish

This chapter concerns itself with the appearance of food rather than with cooking techniques. The material is meant to be studied not for its own sake but for its application to the food preparations that you learn in the rest of your studies. While it may seem very theoretical at first, it has many practical uses.

After studying Chapter 28, you should be able to:

1. Explain why attractive food presentation is important.

2. Serve food that is attractively arranged on the plate or platter, with proper balance of color, shape, and texture.

3. Identify common terms from classical garniture that are still in general use today.

4. Garnish a banquet platter with attractive and appropriate vegetable accompaniments.

5. Plan and arrange attractive food platters for buffets.

A. Terms

Fill in each blank with the term that is defined or described.

_____ 1. To add an edible decorative item to food.

_____ 2. A decorative edible item added to food.

_____ 3. A type of buffet serving only appetizers, usually to accompany drinks.

_____ 4. The centerpiece of a cold buffet platter.

_____ 5. An oval relish dish.

_____ 6. Bread slices cut into triangles or heart shapes, toasted, and used as garnish.

_____ 7. The four components that make up a plated food arrangement.

_____

_____

_____

B. Garnish Review

In the blanks provided, write the specific food items or ingredients that the garnish terms refer to.

_____ 1. Niçoise

_____ 2. Dubarry

_____ 3. Lyonnaise

_____ 4. Parmentier

_____ 5. Printanière

_____ 6. Judic

_____ 7. Primeurs

_____ 8. Florentine

_____ 9. Princesse

_____ 10. Bouquetière

_____ 11. Doria

_____ 12. Jardinière

_____ 13. Vichy

_____ 14. Forestière

_____ 15. Crécy

_____ 16. Fermière

_____ 17. Clamart

_____ 18. Provençale

C. True/False

T   F   **1.** The main meat or fish item on a plate is always placed in the center.

T   F   **2.** The term garnish sometimes refers to vegetable accompaniments.

T   F   **3.** A T-bone steak should be plated so that the bone is toward the back of the plate, away from the customer.

T   F   **4.** To make the portions look generous, the meat and vegetable items on a plate should be piled up against each other.

T   F   **5.** Every buffet platter requires a centerpiece.

T   F   **6.** Filet mignon plated with various garnishes is listed on the menu as "filet mignon with garni."

T   F   **7.** A simple garnish should always be edible, even if it is not intended to be eaten.

T   F   **8.** Deep-fried foods are usually not suited for chafing-dish service.

T   F   **9.** On a buffet, sauces and dressings should be placed next to the items with which they are to be eaten.

D. Review of Cold Platter Design

Following the principles outlined on pages 887–889 of the text, draw diagrams of food arrangements on each of the four platters outlined below. Develop your own designs; do not copy the examples in Figure 28.1. In the blanks provided, you may indicate what foods you are using. Use your ideas, or whatever food items are assigned by your instructor. (A platter may have more than one main food item and/or more than one garnish; for example, slices of veal pâté and slices of pickled veal tongue as two main items on one platter.)

Centerpiece _____

Main item(s) _____

_____

Garnish(es) _____

_____

Centerpiece _____

Main item(s) _____

_____

Garnish(es) _____

_____

Centerpiece _____

Main item(s) _____

_____

Garnish(es) _____

_____

Centerpiece _____

Main item(s) _____

_____

Garnish(es) _____

_____

Chapter 29

Bakeshop Production: Basic Principles and Ingredients

This is the first of seven chapters dealing with the bakeshop. We begin with some basic principles and an introduction to the primary ingredients used in baking. You will need to understand this material before proceeding to the production chapters.

After studying Chapter 29, you should be able to:

1. Explain why it is important to weigh baking ingredients.
2. Use a baker's balance scale.
3. Calculate formulas based on baker's percentages.
4. Explain the factors that control the development of gluten in baked products.
5. Explain the changes that take place in a dough or batter as it bakes.
6. Prevent or retard the staling of baked items.
7. Describe the major ingredients of baked goods and their functions and characteristics.

A. Terms

Fill in each blank with the term that is defined or described.

_____ 1. The chemical name for regular refined sugar or table sugar.

_____ 2. A flavoring ingredient consisting of flavorful oils mixed with water with the aid of vegetable gums or other substances.

_____   **3.** A substance, made up of proteins present in wheat flour, that gives structure and strength to baked goods.

_____   **4.** Flour with a high protein content, derived from hard wheat.

_____   **5.** Flour with a low protein content, from soft wheat.

_____   **6.** The process by which yeast changes carbohydrates to alcohol and carbon dioxide gas.

_____   **7.** The primary sugar present in corn syrup.

_____   **8.** The rendered fat of hogs.

_____   **9.** The change in texture of baked goods due in part to the loss of moisture by the starch granules.

_____   **10.** A flavoring ingredient consisting of flavorful oils and other substances dissolved in alcohol.

_____   **11.** The product that results when cocoa beans are roasted and ground.

_____   **12.** The white or yellowish fat that is a component of the product described in number 11.

_____   **13.** The dry powder that remains after part of the fat is removed from the product described in number 11.

_____   **14.** The dried powder as described in number 13, but processed with alkali.

_____   **15.** The product that is made when sugar is added to the product described in number 11.

_____   **16.** The product that is made when sugar and milk solids are added to the product described in number 11.

_____   **17.** The production or incorporation of gases in a baked product to increase volume and to produce shape and texture.

_____   **18.** Any of a group of solid fats, usually white and tasteless, that have been especially formulated for baking.

_____   **19.** The process of beating fat and sugar together to incorporate air.

_____   **20.** The process of whipping eggs, with or without sugar, to incorporate air.

_____   **21.** The finest or smoothest variety of confectioners' sugar.

B. Flour Review

Flour is the fundamental raw material of the bakeshop. Define or describe, as thoroughly as you can, each of the following products. If the product is a wheat flour, be sure to indicate whether it is a strong (high-gluten) flour or weak (low-gluten) flour.

1. Cake flour: _____

_____

_____

2. Bread flour: _____

_____

_____

3. Pastry flour: _____

_____

_____

4. Rye flour: _____

_____

_____

5. Pumpernickel: _____

_____

_____

6. Rye meal: _____

_____

_____

7. Patent flour: _____

_____

_____

8. Pastry flour: _____

_____

_____

9. Whole wheat flour: _____

_____

_____

10. Bran flour: _____

_____

_____

11. Rye blend: _____

_____

_____

C. Short-Answer Questions

1. What is the weight of 1 pint of water? _____

2. What other liquid ingredients, commonly used in the bakeshop, weigh the same as water? _____

_____

3. List four factors that influence the development of gluten in doughs and batters.

(a) _____

(b) _____

(c) _____

(d) _____

4. Fresh-baked goods can often become stale quickly. What are three factors that can help slow down the staling process?

(a) _____

(b) _____

(c) _____

5. List five functions of fats in baked goods.

(a) _____

(b) _____

(c) _____

(d) _____

(e) _____

6. List five functions of sugars in baked goods.

(a) _____

(b) _____

(c) _____

(d) _____

(e) _____

7. List eight functions of eggs in baked goods.

(a) _____

(b) _____

(c) _____

(d) _____

(e) _____

(f) _____

(g) _____

(h) _____

8. At what temperatures does yeast grow best? _____

At what temperature is yeast killed? _____

9. What are three functions of salt in baked goods?

(a) _____

(b) _____

(c) _____

D. Using Baker's Percentages

Use the percentages given to calculate the quantities needed in the following formulas. If you normally work with U.S. units of measure, fill in the blanks to the left of the percent column. If you normally work with metric units, fill in the blanks to the right of the percent column. You are provided with either the weight of flour or the total yield by weight.

	U.S.	Percent	Metric
I.			
Butter	_____	80%	_____
Sugar	_____	60%	_____
Salt	_____	1%	_____
Ground almonds	_____	50%	_____
Eggs	_____	16.5%	_____
Pastry flour	5 lb	100%	2500 g
II.			
Butter	_____	90%	_____
Sugar	_____	100%	_____
Sweet chocolate	_____	135%	_____
Egg yolks	_____	100%	_____
Egg whites	_____	150%	_____
Sugar	_____	75%	_____
Cake flour	_____	100%	_____
Yield	2 lb 5.5 oz	750%	1125 g

III.

Pastry flour	3 lb	100%	1500 g
Baking powder		5%	
Baking soda		1.25%	
Salt		1.25%	
Sugar		6.5%	
Butter		10%	
Raisins		20%	
Buttermilk		90%	

Chapter 30

Yeast Products

Bread is perhaps the most important product of the bakeshop. Procedures for making breads and other yeast products are discussed in Chapter 30. To make these products successfully, you must understand how to mix ingredients into doughs, how to control gluten development, and how to control yeast fermentation.

After studying Chapter 30, you should be able to:

1. Prepare breads and dinner rolls.
2. Prepare sweet dough products.
3. Prepare Danish pastry and croissants.

A. Terms

Fill in each blank with the term that is defined or described.

_____ 1. The process by which yeast acts on carbohydrates to produce alcohol and carbon dioxide gas.

_____ 2. The continuation of the yeast action after the dough is shaped into loaves or other products, resulting in increase in volume.

_____ 3. A dough that is low in fat and sugar.

_____ 4. A dough that is high in fat and sugar, and sometimes eggs.

_____ 5. The rapid rising of a yeast dough in the oven due to production and expansion of gases.

_____ 6. A dough in which fat is incorporated into the dough in many layers by using a folding and rolling procedure.

_____ **7.** A yeast dough mixing method in which all ingredients are combined at once.

_____ **8.** A dough that has fermented too long.

_____ **9.** A dough that has not fermented long enough.

_____ **10.** A method of deflating dough to expel carbon dioxide.

_____ **11.** The process of shaping scaled dough into smooth, round balls.

_____ **12.** A crescent-shaped roll made of a rolled-in dough.

_____ **13.** Crumb topping for pastries, made of flour, butter, and sugar.

B. True/False

T   F   **1.** The dough arm attachment is used for mixing most yeast doughs.

T   F   **2.** A well-developed French bread dough should be quite sticky.

T   F   **3.** Club rolls and Parker House rolls are two examples of rolled-in dough products.

T   F   **4.** Punching is done by hitting the dough with your fist.

T   F   **5.** The temperature of a proof box should be set at 75°F (24°C) for most yeast products.

T   F   **6.** When made-up bread loaves are placed in baking pans, seams should be on the bottom.

T   F   **7.** Most breads and rolls are baked at a temperature of about 350°F (175°C).

T   F   **8.** Rich doughs are usually slightly underfermented before punching.

T   F   **9.** Bread in the oven is tested for doneness by testing it with a dough thermometer.

T   F   **10.** To maintain freshness, bread should be stored in the refrigerator.

C. Mixing Yeast Doughs

1. In the space below, write the procedure for mixing yeast doughs by the straight dough method.

2. In the space below, write the procedure for mixing rich yeast doughs by the modified straight dough method.

3. In the space below, write the procedure for mixing yeast doughs by the sponge method.

D. Using Baker's Percentages

Use the percentages given to calculate the quantities needed in the following formula. If you normally work with U.S. units of measure, fill in the blanks to the left of the percent column. If you normally work with metric units, fill in the blanks to the right of the percent column.

	U.S.	Percent	Metric
Milk		30%	
Yeast		5%	
Bread flour	6 oz	30%	175 g
Butter		40%	
Sugar		20%	
Salt		1.25%	
Eggs		35%	
Bread flour	14 oz	70%	425 g
Raisins		12.5%	

Chapter 31

Quick Breads

This chapter deals with products that are not only very popular but also very easy to make. Consequently, this will be useful information to you in your career, so you should study it well. After studying Chapter 31, you should be able to:

1. Prepare baking powder biscuits and variations.
2. Prepare muffins, loaf breads, coffee cakes, and corn breads.
3. Prepare popovers.

A. Terms

Fill in each blank with the term that is defined or described.

_____ 1. The development of elongated holes inside muffin products.

_____ 2. A batter that is liquid enough to be poured.

_____ 3. A batter that is too thick to be poured, but that will drop from a spoon in lumps.

_____ 4. A baked product made of a thin batter, leavened only by steam, and characterized by very large holes on the inside.

B. Review of Mixing Methods

1. In the space below, write the procedure for mixing doughs by the biscuit method.

2. In the space below, write the procedure for mixing batters by the muffin method.

C. Using Baker's Percentages

Use the percentages given to calculate the quantities needed in the following formula. If you normally work with U.S. units of measure, fill in the blanks to the left of the percent column. If you normally work with metric units, fill in the blanks to the right of the percent column.

	U.S.	Percent	Metric
Pastry flour	_____	100%	_____
Sugar	_____	40%	_____
Baking powder	_____	5%	_____
Baking soda	_____	0.6%	_____
Salt	_____	1.25%	_____
Walnuts	_____	25%	_____
Eggs	_____	40%	_____
Banana pulp	_____	90%	_____
Melted butter	_____	33%	_____
Yield	7 lb 8 oz	334%	3348 g

Chapter 32

Cakes and Icings

Because cakes are such delicate products, mixing and baking them requires a great deal of precision and care. It is important, then, that you study and review this chapter thoroughly in order to make superior cakes.

After studying Chapter 32, you should be able to:

1. Demonstrate the five basic cake mixing methods.
2. Describe the characteristics of high-fat cakes and low-fat cakes.
3. Prepare high-fat, or shortened, cakes and low-fat, or foam-type, cakes.
4. Prepare the six basic types of icings.
5. Assemble and ice layer cakes, small cakes, and sheet cakes.

A. Terms

Fill in each blank with the term that is defined or described.

_____ 1. A type of cake based on an egg-white foam and containing no fat.

_____ 2. A type of cake made with an egg-white foam and oil.

_____ 3. A classic cake made of equal parts butter, sugar, flour, and eggs.

_____ 4. A classic sponge cake made of eggs, sugar, flour, and melted butter, but with no other liquid.

_____ 5. An icing made by creaming together fat and sugar.

_____ 6. An icing made by mixing confectioners' sugar and egg whites.

_____ **7.** An icing that consists of a sugar syrup that has been crystallized to a smooth, creamy white mass.

_____ **8.** An icing that consists primarily of confectioners' sugar mixed with water.

_____ **9.** A glossy, transparent coating that gives a shine to baked products.

B. Review of Cake Mixing Methods

1. In the space below, explain how to mix cakes by the creaming method. Be sure to include all the necessary steps, and number the steps.

2. In the space below, explain how to mix cakes by the two-stage method. Be sure to include all the necessary steps, and number the steps.

3. In the space below, explain how to mix angel food cakes. Be sure to include all the necessary steps, and number the steps.

4. In the space below, explain how to mix genoise-type sponge cakes. Include all the necessary steps, and number the steps.

5. In the space below, explain how to mix chiffon cakes. Write the procedure in the form of numbered steps.

C. Review of Icing Preparations

1. Fondant must be warmed for use, but it should not be heated above 100°F (38°C). Why? _____

_____

2. How do you make chocolate fondant? _____

_____

3. Name and describe the three main types of buttercream.

(a) _____

_____

(b) _____

_____

(c) _____

_____

4. What is decorator's buttercream? _____

_____

_____

5. What is royal icing used for? _____

6. Briefly describe how to make and how to store royal icing.

_____

_____

_____

_____

7. Briefly describe two methods for icing cupcakes.

(a) _____

_____

(b) _____

_____

8. Flat icings are handled and applied in the same way as what other type of icing? _____

_____

9. What is a foam icing? _____

_____

D. Using Baker's Percentages

Use the percentages given to calculate the quantities needed in the following formula. If you normally work with U.S. units of measure, fill in the blanks to the left of the percent column. If you normally work with metric units, fill in the blanks to the right of the percent column.

	U.S.	Percent	Metric
Flour	_____	100%	_____
Salt	_____	2%	_____
Baking powder	_____	2%	_____
Emulsified shortening	_____	67%	_____
Sugar	_____	117%	_____
Nonfat milk solids	_____	6%	_____
Water	_____	45%	_____
Eggs	_____	67%	_____
Raisins	_____	25%	_____
Yield	8 lb 8 oz	430%	3865 g

Chapter 33

Cookies

Like most kitchen and bakeshop tasks, learning to make cookies easily and efficiently is primarily a matter of developing manual skills. But like most food service tasks, it also requires some understanding of theory and basic principles. This chapter will help you review those principles.

After studying Chapter 33, you should be able to:

1. List the factors responsible for crispness, softness, chewiness, and spread in cookies.

2. Demonstrate the three basic cookie mixing methods.

3. Prepare the seven basic cookies types: dropped, bagged, rolled, molded, icebox, bar, and sheet.

4. Prepare pans for, bake, and cool cookies.

A. Terms

Fill in each blank with the term that is defined or described.

_____ 1. Readily absorbing moisture.

_____ 2. A cookie made of coconut mixed with meringue.

_____ 3. A rich, rather crumbly Scottish cookie made of butter, flour, and sugar; some variations also contain egg.

_____ 4. Finger-shaped soft cookies made from a sponge batter.

The following terms refer to categories of cookies based on makeup method.

_____   **5.** Cookies cut from refrigerated, sausage-shaped pieces of dough.

_____   **6.** Cookies pressed from a pastry bag.

_____   **7.** Cookies made with a cookie cutter.

_____   **8.** Cookies made by spreading dough or batter in sheet pans, baking, and then cutting out squares or rectangles.

_____   **9.** Cookies made from lumps of dough dropped onto baking pans.

_____   **10.** Cookies made from cylinders of dough flattened onto sheet pans, baked, then cut crosswise into pieces.

_____   **11.** Cookies made from equal pieces of dough cut from a cylinder, placed on sheet pans, then pressed flat.

B. Review of Cookie Mixing Methods

1. Using numbered steps, describe the creaming method for mixing cookies.

2. Using numbered steps, describe the one-stage method for mixing cookies.

C. Short-Answer Questions

1. A cookie dough is more likely to spread when baked if its content of granulated sugar is _____ .

2. The main reason for shaping cookies uniformly during makeup is _____ .

3. Cookie dough to be rolled out with a rolling pin should be at what temperature? _____

4. What is likely to happen to cookies baked at too high a temperature? _____

5. What should be done with freshly baked cookies before they are put in containers for storage? _____

_____

6. How much flour should be used for dusting when rolling out cookie dough with a rolling pin? _____

_____

7. What is the main indication of doneness when cookies are baked? _____

8. If a rich cookie dough burns too easily when baked, what can be done to prevent burning? _____

_____

D. Using Baker's Percentages

Use the percentages given to calculate the quantities needed in the following formula. If you normally work with U.S. units of measure, fill in the blanks to the left of the percent column. If you normally work with metric units, fill in the blanks to the right of the percent column.

	U.S.	Percent	Metric
Butter	_____	67%	_____
Brown sugar	_____	133%	_____
Salt	_____	1.5%	_____
Eggs	_____	33%	_____
Vanilla	_____	3%	_____
Milk	_____	8%	_____
Pastry flour	1 lb 14 oz	100%	900 g
Baking powder	_____	4%	_____
Baking soda	_____	2%	_____
Rolled oats	_____	83%	_____
Raisins	_____	50%	_____

Chapter 34

Pies and Pastries

Many kinds of products are presented in Chapter 34, and the techniques used to prepare them are important ones. The various review exercises here will help you study the various procedures involved in pastry making.

After studying Chapter 34, you should be able to:

1. Prepare flaky pie dough and mealy pie dough.
2. Prepare crumb crusts and short, or cookie, crusts.
3. Assemble and bake pies.
4. Prepare the following pie fillings: fruit fillings using the cooked juice method, the cooked fruit method, and the old-fashioned method; custard or soft fillings; cream pie fillings; and chiffon fillings.
5. Prepare puff pastry dough and puff dough products.
6. Prepare éclair paste and éclair paste products.
7. Prepare standard meringues and meringue desserts.
8. Prepare fruit desserts.

A. Terms

Fill in each blank with the term that is defined or described.

_____ 1. A type of dough that is mixed like pie dough but rolled and folded like puff paste.

_____ 2. A dessert consisting of ice cream covered with meringue and browned in the oven.

_____ 3. Starch that thickens liquids without cooking, because it has been precooked.

_____ **4.** A dessert made of layers of puff pastry alternating with layers of pastry cream or other cream.

_____ **5.** French name for eclair paste.

_____ **6.** A type of meringue made with boiling syrup.

_____ **7.** Tiny cream puffs, often filled with ice cream and served with chocolate syrup.

_____ **8.** A type of meringue made with a warmed mixture of egg whites and sugar.

_____ **9.** A type of pie filling that is lightened by the addition of whipped egg whites.

_____ **10.** A starch that makes a clear gel when cooked and that does not break down when frozen.

_____ **11.** A crisp disk of baked meringue containing nuts.

_____ **12.** A baked dessert made of sliced, sugared apples topped with a crumb or streussel topping flavored with cinnamon.

_____ **13.** A baked meringue shell filled with ice cream.

_____ **14.** Baking a pie or tart shell without a filling.

B. Pie Review

1. The main types of pie dough are _____ and _____ .

2. The difference between the two main types of pie dough mostly depends on _____

_____ .

3. Water for pie dough should be at what temperature? _____

4. What are two functions of salt in pie dough? _____

_____

_____

5. If shortening is used to make pie dough, what type of shortening is the correct one to use? _____

_____

6. The two basic steps in the rubbed dough method are _____

_____

7. A basic graham cracker crust is made with what ingredients?

_____

8. Assume you have made a fruit pie filling by the cooked juice method. At about what temperature should the filling be when the pie shell is filled? _____

9. Vanilla cream pie filling is thickened with _____ .

10. The best thickening agent to use for fruit pie fillings is _____ .

11. To prevent lumping, starch must be mixed with _____ or with _____ before being added to a hot liquid.

12. In the space below, list the four ingredients in basic pie dough, then write the procedure for mixing the ingredients to make a dough. Use numbered steps. Be sure to explain the difference between the two main types of dough.

    Ingredients: _____

    _____

    _____

    _____

    Procedure:

13. In the space below, explain how to make fruit pie fillings using the cooked juice method. Write the procedure in the form of numbered steps.

14. In the space below, explain how to make fruit pie fillings using the cooked fruit method. Write the procedure in the form of numbered steps.

C. True/False

T   F   **1.** Eclair paste is made with pastry flour.

T   F   **2.** Puff paste is rolled and folded with the same number of folds as Danish pastry.

T   F   **3.** Puff pastry is leavened with baking powder.

T   F   **4.** Eclair paste is leavened with baking soda.

T   F   **5.** Puff paste is refrigerated briefly between turns, especially if the bakeshop is warm.

T   F   **6.** Butter to be rolled into puff paste must be well chilled and hard so that it won't ooze out of the dough.

T   F   **7.** A 4-fold gets its name because it results in four times as many layers in the dough each time it is done.

T   F   **8.** Eclairs are baked at a low temperature to give them time to puff up.

T   F   **9.** The flour mixture for eclair paste is chilled before the eggs are added.

T   F   **10.** Hard meringues are baked at a low temperature so that they will dry out but will not brown.

T   F   **11.** Meringue pie topping is made with about 4 oz of sugar per pound of egg whites (250 g sugar per kilogram of egg whites).

D. Using Baker's Percentages

Use the percentages given to calculate the quantities needed in the following formulas. If you normally work with U.S. units of measure, fill in the blanks to the left of the percent column. If you normally work with metric units, fill in the blanks to the right of the percent column. You are provided with either the weight of flour or the total yield by weight.

	U.S.	Percent	Metric
I.			
Pastry flour	_____	100%	_____
Shortening	_____	70%	_____
Salt	_____	2%	_____
Water	_____	30%	_____
Yield	_____14 lb_____	202%	_____6000 g_____

II.

Pastry flour	4 lb	100%	2000 g	
Sugar		17%		
Butter		50%		
Egg yolks		8%		
Water		25%		
Salt		1%		

Chapter 35

Creams, Custards, Puddings, Frozen Desserts, and Sauces

Like the previous chapter, this chapter presents a wide variety of techniques and products. Some of these products, like pastry cream, are used as components of many different kinds of desserts and pastries, so it is important to know them well. Since many of the recipes are based on egg custards, it will also help you to review what you learned about eggs in Chapter 24.

After studying Chapter 35, you should be able to:

1. Cook sugar syrups to the seven stages of hardness.
2. Prepare crème anglaise, pastry cream, and baked custard.
3. Prepare starch-thickened puddings and baked puddings.
4. Prepare bavarians, chiffons, mousses, and dessert soufflés.
5. Assemble frozen desserts.
6. Prepare dessert sauces.

A. Terms

Fill in each blank with the term that is defined or described.

_____ 1. A custard sauce made of sweetened, vanilla-flavored milk thickened with egg yolks.

_____ 2. A flavored simple syrup, used to moisten and flavor some cakes.

_____ 3. A thick stirred custard thickened with starch as well as with eggs; used as a pastry and pie filling and as a pudding.

_____   **4.** A baked custard made in a caramel-lined mold, so that it has a caramel topping when turned out of the mold.

_____   **5.** A white cornstarch pudding, often flavored with almond extract.

_____   **6.** A pudding similar to a cornstarch pudding but also containing eggs.

_____   **7.** A dessert consisting of alternating layers of ice cream and fruit or syrup in a tall, narrow glass.

_____   **8.** Ice cream containing no eggs.

_____   **9.** The increase in volume of ice cream during freezing due to incorporation of air.

_____   **10.** A chilled dessert made of flavored custard sauce, gelatin, and whipped cream.

_____   **11.** A soft or creamy dessert made light or fluffy by the addition of whipped cream or whipped egg whites or both.

_____   **12.** A dessert consisting of one or two scoops of ice cream or sherbet in a dish or glass, topped with any of a number of syrups, fruits, or toppings.

_____   **13.** A molded ice cream dessert consisting of two or more layers of different ice creams.

_____   **14.** A baked, pudding-like dessert lightened with whipped egg whites.

_____   **15.** A frozen dessert similar to ice cream but with a lower butterfat content.

_____   **16.** A dessert consisting of a pear half, chocolate sauce, and toasted almonds on top of vanilla ice cream.

_____   **17.** A frozen dessert made of fruit juices, water, sugar, and sometimes egg whites, but containing no milk products.

_____   **18.** A frozen dessert similar to the one described in number 17 but with a coarse, crystalline texture and made without egg whites.

_____   **19.** A dessert or pie filling containing gelatin and whipped egg whites.

_____   **20.** A dessert consisting of a peach half and raspberry sauce on top of vanilla ice cream.

_____   **21.** The browning of sugar caused by heat.

B. Review of Sugar Cooking

1. A simple syrup is a solution of equal parts _____ and _____ .

2. Dessert syrup is a simple syrup plus _____ .

3. When a syrup is boiled, moisture gradually evaporates, and the temperature of the syrup gradually _____ .

4. If a syrup is cooked to 300°F (150°C) and then cooled, its texture will be _____ .

5. If a syrup is cooked until it turns light brown, the resulting product is called _____ .

6. If an acid, such as _____ , is added to a syrup before cooking, some of the sugar turns

   to _____ . The advantage of this is _____

   _____ .

7. When you want to cook a syrup to a certain stage of doneness, the tool you need to accurately test for doneness

   is _____ .

8. When the instructions in a candy recipe say to "wash down the sides of the pan with a brush dipped in water,"

   the purpose of this direction is _____

   _____ .

C. Review of Basic Custards and Creams

1. The basic ingredients of crème anglaise are _____ , _____ ,

   _____ , and vanilla.

2. Crème anglaise is completely cooked when it reaches a temperature of _____ .

3. Why is a double boiler generally used to make crème anglaise? _____

   _____

4. Why is it important to use clean, sanitary equipment when making crème anglaise and pastry cream?

_____

_____

5. Why is it important to chill pastry cream quickly after it is cooked? _____

_____

6. After pastry cream is cooked, it is poured into _____ pans so that it will cool quickly.

7. What is the advantage of baking custards in a hot-water bath? _____

_____

8. When making baked custards, what is the advantage of scalding the milk before adding it to the eggs?

_____

_____

9. In the space below, write the procedure for preparing crème anglaise. Use numbered steps.

10. In the space that follows, write the procedure for preparing vanilla pastry cream.

D. True/False

T   F   **1.** Lemon pie filling is made using the same technique as vanilla pastry cream.

T   F   **2.** A boiling syrup that is at the crack stage is hotter than a boiling syrup at the hard ball stage.

T   F   **3.** Corn syrup should not be added to a boiling sugar syrup because it may cause crystallization.

T   F   **4.** French-style ice cream contains egg yolks.

T   F   **5.** For sanitary reasons, crème anglaise should be brought to a boil to kill bacteria.

T   F   **6.** When scalded milk is added to egg yolks, it should be added all at once.

T   F   **7.** A dessert soufflé is always baked at a low temperature (about 300°F/150°C) to give the soufflé time to rise properly.

T   F   **8.** If both whipped cream and whipped egg whites must be added to a chocolate mousse, the whipped cream is always added first.

T   F   **9.** If egg whites for a dessert soufflé are beaten with some sugar, this helps to make the soufflé more stable.

T   F   **10.** Butterscotch pudding is made by making vanilla pudding with extra butter, and adding scotch flavoring.

T   F   **11.** Frozen mousses can be still-frozen (not churn-frozen in an ice cream freezer) because they contain whipped cream or whipped egg whites.

T   F   **12.** A coupe is basically the same as a sundae.

E. Portion Cost

Cost out the following recipe. For prices of the ingredients, use figures supplied by your instructor or the *Sample Prices* in the Appendix of this *Study Guide*.

ITEM: **CHOCOLATE CREAM PIE**

Ingredient	Recipe Quantity	AP Quantity	Price	Total Amount
Flour	12 oz	_____	_____	_____
Shortening	8 oz	_____	_____	_____
Water	4 oz	_____	_____	_____
Milk	2 qt	_____	_____	_____
Sugar	1 lb	_____	_____	_____
Eggs	8	_____	_____	_____
Cornstarch	5 oz	_____	_____	_____
Sweet chocolate	4 oz	_____	_____	_____
Bitter chocolate	4 oz	_____	_____	_____
Butter	4 oz	_____	_____	_____
Vanilla	1 oz	_____	_____	_____

Total cost _____

Number of portions   24

Cost per portion _____

Portion Cost—Metric

Cost out the following recipe. For prices of the ingredients, use figures supplied by your instructor or the *Sample Prices* in the Appendix of this *Study Guide*.

ITEM: **CHOCOLATE CREAM PIE**

Ingredient	Recipe Quantity	AP Quantity	Price	Total Amount
Flour	375 g	_____	_____	_____
Shortening	250 g	_____	_____	_____
Water	125 g	_____	_____	_____
Milk	2 L	_____	_____	_____
Sugar	500 g	_____	_____	_____
Eggs	8	_____	_____	_____
Cornstarch	150 g	_____	_____	_____
Sweet chocolate	125 g	_____	_____	_____
Bitter chocolate	125 g	_____	_____	_____
Butter	125 g	_____	_____	_____
Vanilla	30 mL	_____	_____	_____

Total cost _____

Number of portions 24

Cost per portion _____

Appendix: Sample Prices

Your instructors may want you to use the prices on current invoices when you do the Portion Cost exercises in this manual. If not, you may use the following hypothetical prices. Do not worry about whether or not these prices seem realistic. Prices change, but you can still practice the calculations with these numbers.

Meat, Poultry, and Fish

Beef brisket	$ 1.80 per lb	$ 3.89 per kg
Beef, ground	1.39 per lb	3.19 per kg
Chicken parts	0.85 per lb	1.85 per kg
Italian pork sausages	1.49 per lb	3.29 per kg
Sole fillets	5.99 per lb	13.00 per kg

Produce and Frozen Vegetables

Artichokes	$ 0.45 each	$ 0.45 each
Cabbage	0.25 per lb	0.55 per kg
Carrots	0.30 per lb	0.65 per kg
Leeks	1.10 per lb	2.40 per kg
Lemons	0.20 each	0.20 each
Lettuce, iceberg	0.80 per head	0.80 per head
Mushrooms	1.25 per lb	2.75 per kg
Onions, yellow	0.30 per lb	0.65 per kg
Peas, frozen	2.20 per 2½ lb pack	1.95 per kg
Peppers, green bell	0.50 per lb	1.15 per kg
Peppers, red bell	2.49 per lb	5.49 per kg
Peppers, Italian	0.80 per lb	1.75 per kg
Potatoes, all-purpose	0.20 per lb	0.45 per kg
Potatoes, baking, "100's" (8-oz average weight)	0.30 per lb	0.65 per kg
Shallots	1.50 per lb	3.50 per kg
Squash, butternut	0.35 per lb	0.75 per kg
Tomatoes	0.50 per lb	1.20 per kg

Dairy and Eggs

Butter	$ 1.70 per lb	$ 3.75 per kg
Milk	0.45 per qt	0.45 per L
Heavy cream	2.69 per qt	2.69 per L
Sour cream	1.09 per lb	2.40 per kg
Cheese, Gruyère	4.00 per lb	8.50 per kg
Cheese, Parmesan	6.00 per lb	13.00 per kg
Eggs, large	0.89 per dozen	0.89 per dozen

Groceries

Beets, canned	$ 0.60 per #2½ can	$ 0.60 per #2½ can
Breadcrumbs, dry	0.79 per lb	1.79 per kg
Bulgur wheat	0.79 per lb	1.79 per kg
Chili powder	0.75 per oz	2.70 per 100 g
Chocolate, bitter	3.98 per lb	8.79 per kg
Chocolate, sweet	3.69 per lb	8.19 per kg
Cornstarch	0.59 per lb	1.29 per kg
Flour	0.15 per lb	0.35 per kg
Ginger, ground	1.40 per oz	5.00 per 100 g
Mayonnaise	6.50 per gal	1.65 per L
Oil, olive	3.29 per qt	3.29 per L
Oil, salad/vegetable	4.60 per gal	1.20 per L
Pepper, black	0.45 per oz	1.59 per 100 g
Raisins	1.09 per lb	2.39 per kg
Salt	0.15 per lb	0.35 per kg
Shortening	0.55 per lb	1.20 per kg
Soy sauce	1.25 per pt	2.50 per L
Spaghetti	0.79 per lb	1.75 per kg
Sugar, brown	0.45 per lb	1.00 per kg
Sugar, granulated	0.30 per lb	0.65 per kg
Tomato paste	0.70 per 1-lb can	0.75 per 500-g can
Tomato purée	0.45 per 1-lb can	0.50 per 500-g can
Tomatoes, whole, canned	0.35 per lb	0.75 per kg
Tomatoes, #10 can	2.10 per can	2.10 per can
Vanilla	10.00 per qt	10.00 per L
Vinegar, red wine	0.75 per qt	0.75 per L

Miscellaneous

Beef stock	$ 0.30 per qt	$ 0.30 per L
Chicken stock	0.25 per qt	0.25 per L
Fish stock	0.50 per qt	0.50 per L
Sherry wine	7.00 per qt	7.00 per L